THE RICHNESS OF CHRIST

J. A. MOTYER

THE RICHNESS OF CHRIST

STUDIES IN THE LETTER TO THE PHILIPPIANS

INTER-VARSITY FELLOWSHIP
39 BEDFORD SQUARE, LONDON WC1

First Edition March 1966

*Printed by Staples Printers Ltd.
at their Rochester, Kent, establishment*

CONTENTS

TO RAYMOND AND MURIEL

PREFACE

These studies in the Epistle to the Philippians were first prepared in 1962 for the Autumn Session of the Prince's Hall Bible School, Bristol. They were then expanded for the weekly Bible Reading in the chapel of Clifton Theological College, and were further used at the morning Bible Readings at Webster Memorial Church, Kingston, Jamaica, in the course of the 1965 Kingston Convention. I would like to thank all these different groups for their patience as I attempted to say again what Paul has already said, and for their encouragement, and their helpful discussion of individual points.

I am, of course, deeply indebted to the commentators, and it may provide a reading guide for further study of Philippians if I say that I derived greatest profit from the following, some of which are occasionally quoted in these studies: Calvin, Bengel (*Gnomon of the New Testament*), Alford (*Greek Testament*), Martin (*Tyndale New Testament Commentary*), Vincent (*International Critical Commentary*), Vaughan (*Lectures on Philippians*), Lightfoot, Moule (*Cambridge Bible,* referred to as *CB,* and *Philippian Studies,* referred to as *PS*), and Hendriksen (*Geneva Commentary*).

In my own study, I used the Revised Version, which is, in my opinion, the best available version for study purposes. In the interests of avoiding unnecessary archaisms, and of conforming to increasing present practice, quotations have been made throughout from the Revised Standard Version. Occasionally, however, my preference for the RV peeps through, and I must beg the reader's pardon in advance for those few places where some tension between the versions is apparent.

My object in this book may be stated in words already used: 'to say again what Paul has already said'. The reader will not find himself made the object of much exhortation, nor will he find himself over-involved in what is sometimes called 'devotional application'. Indeed, I have occasionally queried whether perhaps a chapter does not end too abruptly, and whether enough has been said to prompt in the reader the questions which have posed themselves to the author: 'What about me? Is this true of me? Can I claim this promise for myself? Does Christ mean as much to me as this?' But the task of exposition is to open up what is there in the Bible, and to go extensively beyond that task is sometimes to risk suggesting to the reader problems which are not in fact his, and thus to raise false anxieties. On the other hand, to state what the Bible states and to invite the reader, with the writer, to take the matter on to the next stage for himself is to honour that great Christian doctrine, the equality of believers before the Word of God.

Philippians speaks at many points to our present situation, and not least, for example, in its teaching on the pressing question of Christian unity. But I have found its pressure to be most intense upon my own soul at the point reflected in the over-all title of these studies. Christ meant simply everything to Paul, and Paul wrote in order to share 'the surpassing worth of knowing Christ Jesus my Lord' with his friends, who now include you and me. To me, and possibly to you, such knowledge of the richness of Christ is an aspiration rather than a fact, but an aspiration which, please God, and maybe through the perusal of these pages, will henceforth be daily more and more an experienced reality.

St Luke's Vicarage, Hampstead J. A. MOTYER
November 1965

1 THE CHRISTIAN DEFINED

IT SOUNDS STRANGE TO US that Paul should address his readers not as Philippians but as 'the saints . . . who are at Philippi'. The strangeness, of course, consists in the fact that for the most part modern usage would lead us to expect '*Saint* Paul . . . to the Christians at Philippi', and not '*Slave* Paul to the *saints* at Philippi'. Throughout the New Testament, however, 'saints' is the customary description of the ordinary Christian believer. The word 'Christian' in fact occurs only three times in the New Testament, whereas on over sixty occasions we find the word 'saint'. A very striking example of this is supplied by 1 Corinthians 1: 2 where 'the church of God which is at Corinth' is defined as consisting of 'those sanctified in Christ Jesus, called to be saints'. That is to say, the church is a divine possession; it has a local manifestation; its members are such by virtue of what Christ has done for them, and in consequence of which they possess a glorious title, 'saints'.

Now the present section of Philippians is no less definite. Paul is occupied here with his opening greeting, but if we try to penetrate beneath what he is doing and ask what, by implication, he is teaching, nothing will satisfy the content of these verses so well as to say that he is here defining what a Christian is, and that at the heart of the definition lies this familiar word, 'saint'.

I THE CHRISTIAN'S TITLE

What is implied by calling the Christian a saint? The word itself means 'holy', and when we grasp this we are well on our way to seeing that in this title the essential greatness of our privilege as Christians is expressed. But in order to see this we must gather evidence from outside the Epistle to the Philippians. Luke 1: 35 gives us a dramatic introduction to the real bearing of the word 'holy'. It reads, 'The Holy Spirit will come upon you, and the power of the Most High will overshadow you; therefore the child to be born will be called holy, the Son of God.' The 'power of the Most High' is 'the *Holy* Spirit'; the 'Son of God' is the '*holy*' child. 'Holy' is the word above all others which the Bible uses to describe God. 'I know who you are,' said the demon-possessed man, 'the Holy One of God' (Lk. 4: 34). 'How much more', said Jesus, 'will the heavenly Father give the Holy Spirit to those who ask him?' (Lk. 11: 13).

Central to the whole Bible, on this topic, is Isaiah 6: 3, 'Holy, holy, holy is the Lord of hosts.' Isaiah had just been introduced into the very presence of God. He was made aware of the throne and its Occupant (verse 1), the attendants (verse 2), and their song (verse 3). We are probably correct in thinking that Isaiah grasped here the eternity of the rule of God, in contrast with the dying or recently dead Uzziah. The exalted position of the divine King caught his attention, stressing the supremacy of God over all. The song of the seraphim declared the universality of the dominion of Him whose glory fills all the earth. Thus, God is eternal, transcendent, omnipresent; but at the heart of this cluster of divine attributes lies that upon which the seraphim dwelt with an insistent emphasis, 'Holy, holy, holy is the Lord of hosts.' Whatever else may be stated or inferred about God, whatever multiplicity or variety of attributes or descriptions may be necessary, this is always true, that He is the Holy One, and of such perfect and complete holiness that the adjective must be repeated and then repeated again, so that the triple ascription may draw all eyes to, and display the uniqueness of, the essential divine nature.

It is a further indication of the special association of holiness with God that His name is described in the Bible as 'his holy name' more often than all other descriptions ('his great name', 'his fearful name', *etc.*) added together. The Bible thus insists that God is the Holy One. Holiness is the most intimately divine word the Bible possesses. This word touches the very essence of the nature of God in a way that no other does. And it is this word which is now made to describe the Christian!

How easy it would have been for Paul to address himself to the 'Philippians', as he does in 4: 15. But this is not his purpose. His interest as he writes his apostolic message to them is not what or where they are by nature, but what they have become by grace and the position they now occupy in the sight of God. Politically they are Philippians, and no small honour attached to this (Acts 16: 12), but grace has made them nothing less than partakers of the divine nature: the honour of honours, that the Holy God should give His title and His character to men, calling them 'saints'.

II THE CHRISTIAN'S LORD

'Not what they are by nature, but what they have become by grace.' The words we have just used to describe how the Philippians became 'saints' are an apt enough summary of the explanation which Paul gives when he calls them, not 'saints', but 'saints in Christ Jesus'. No such thing as self-effort, or self-improvement is allowed here. The explanation of the Christian's position as a saint involves a pointing away from him and a pointing solely to Christ.

The exclusive position which the Lord Jesus Christ occupies in relation to the Christian possesses three distinct aspects, which Paul here teaches by the words 'in', 'of' and 'from'. The Christian is a saint 'in Christ Jesus', a 'servant of Christ Jesus', and the recipient of 'grace . . . and peace from . . . the Lord Jesus Christ'.

a. The foundation on which the Christian stands

Paul uses the phrase 'in Christ' as a comprehensive description of the Christian, touching every aspect of what God has done for him, and of what he now enjoys, and of the prospect opening out before him in time and eternity. In the present passage, however, we learn nothing but the fact that 'in Christ' we have become 'saints'. Paul does not pause here to describe ways and means. We must therefore call another passage of Scripture briefly to our aid. Ephesians 1, more than any other, uses the words 'in Christ' to point to those great acts of God by which men receive the title and become partakers of the nature of God.

According to Ephesians 1: 3 God the Father has bestowed upon us every sort of spiritual blessing 'in Christ'. When Paul begins to itemize these blessings, he starts (verse 4) with the fact that we were chosen in Christ before the foundation of the world, with the express purpose 'that we should be holy', or 'saints'. No doubt many problems gather round this notion of a divine choice antedating creation, but there is a stark and almost elementary simplicity about the idea itself, and an incredible wonder. To be sure, it is wonderful to remember the day of one's conversion; to recall with what simplicity faith laid hold upon Jesus for salvation. But there is more to becoming a child of God than that, and the over-plus is more amazing and glorious by far. 'You did not choose me,' said Jesus, 'but I chose you' (Jn. 15: 16), and this divine initiative in choosing took place not only before I had any being, but before the world was! Here is the foundation and fount of all further blessedness, and it happened 'in Christ'.

Secondly, the eternal counsel of God became an historical reality at Calvary, where (Eph. 1: 7) in Christ 'we have redemption through his blood, the forgiveness of our trespasses'. The purpose of God to make us 'saints' involved no effort of ours, but the costly act of Christ dying in our place. There could be no holiness where there is sin, and the making of sinners into saints demands such a dealing with sin as only God could bring to pass, forgiveness by the blood of Christ. It is appropriate to our study to recall the words of Hebrews 10: 10 on this point, 'By that will (*i.e.* by the will of the Father) we have been sanctified (given the title and nature of saints) through the offering of the body of Jesus Christ once for all.' Calvary, or rather the Christ of Calvary, has wrought for us a full salvation, both, on the negative side, clearing us of trespasses, and, on the positive side, making us saints.

Thirdly, what was eternal in the plan of God, and historical in the blood of Christ, becomes contemporary through the Holy Spirit, for 'in Christ', when we believed, we were 'sealed with the promised Holy Spirit' (Eph. 1: 13). Thus, indeed, we were made saints, partakers of the divine nature. God the Holy Spirit took up residence in us, setting the seal of divine ownership upon us by His presence. And this, too, was 'in Christ', for the whole plan of salvation is summed up in Him, and transacted in Him, and enjoyed in Him, and 'no other foundation can anyone lay than that which is laid, which is Jesus Christ' (1 Cor. 3: 11). Correctly, therefore, Paul describes the Philippians as 'saints in Christ Jesus'.

b. The Lord whom the Christian serves

There is an interesting parallel in Romans 1: 6,7 between the phrases 'called to belong to Jesus Christ' and 'called to be saints'. When, 'in Christ', a person becomes a saint, an element of loyalty or of ownership is involved. The saint is possessed by Christ, and gladly acknowledges that this is so. Paul declares as much when he describes himself and Timothy here in Philippians as 'servants of Christ Jesus'.

The phrase he actually uses is somewhat stronger, 'slaves of Christ Jesus'. The slave, 'bought with a price' (1 Cor. 6: 20), is absolutely at the disposal of the purchaser to do his bidding. A self-willed, or idle, or disobedient slave is a contradiction in terms. There is, of course, nothing 'servile' about the saint. He is a free man, freed from the bondage and degradation of sin. He is now a man for the first time, for as Christ alone is true Man, so those who are newly alive in Christ are more truly human than they were before. But the saint is an obedient man. Great though his privileges are they do not constitute a dressing-gown and slippers, but a staff and shoes for pilgrimage, and armour for battle, and a plough for the field. Responsive obedience is the mark of the 'saint in Christ Jesus' who is necessarily also 'servant of Christ Jesus'.

None can evade this responsibility. Paul, the apostle, sets himself here on no pedestal of distinctiveness. Though in no sense is Timothy the co-author of the letter, for throughout Paul incessantly uses the 'I' and 'my' of individual experience, yet here Paul and Timothy are one, and the Philippians are one with them, for, as verse 7 says, 'you are all partakers with me of grace'. Christ makes different appointments in His church—some to be apostles, some to be Timothies, some to be overseers, some to be deacons—but none are in the church at all except by grace, and none can partake of grace and fight shy of service. The '*in* Christ' of gracious salvation, if it is real, issues in the '*of* Christ' of responsive, obedient service.

c. The Giver from whom the Christian receives

However, a question naturally arises at this point. Where does the ability to fulfil this duty of service and to live the life of an obedient saint come from? Paul's answer is in two parts. In the first place he lifts our eyes to the greatness of the Lord Jesus. In the Old Testament, Moses and the prophets were given a title of great honour, 'servants of the Lord'. It is not accidental, therefore, that Paul designates himself a 'servant of Christ Jesus', for here as 'everywhere in the Epistles . . . the attitude of Paul towards Christ is not merely the attitude of man to man, or scholar to master; it is the attitude of man towards God' (Machen, quoted by Martin). This is further borne out by the phrase 'from God our Father and the Lord Jesus Christ'. The one preposition 'from' governing both Names has the effect of binding them together to form the single Source of the blessings indicated; the Father and the Lord, the divine Fount from which the saint is supplied.

The supply itself consists of 'grace and peace'. Undoubtedly these are related to each other as cause and effect, and this will be most easily seen if we look at them first in the matter of our salvation. 'Grace' is God being gracious, adopting an attitude and an activity of all-sufficient favour towards helpless and merit-less sinners; God coming to them in free, unprovoked love to give them the opposite of their deservings. 'The riches of his grace' is, in fact, our 'redemption through his blood' (Eph. 1: 7), and the first-fruits of this is peace with God, even as Jesus Himself declared when He came to the shut-in disciples on the first Easter, saying 'Peace be with you' (Jn. 20: 19,21). Grace produced reconciliation.

When Paul wishes these blessings for Christians, he is not desiring their salvation all over again, though the blessings are those of salvation. First, he is assuring them of the unchanged regard of God: the God who planned and accomplished and freely gave salvation is the same God who in like grace gives every needful thing to His people. And just as the initiative of God in grace brought peace to sinners, so grace always precedes peace, for God is always taking the initiative to act on behalf of His own and to keep them in possession of the blessings of peace, spiritual well-being, which He purchased for them with the blood of His Son. The saint is not left to walk the path of obedience alone. The saving God remains the same. The provision of salvation is available at all times. Grace and peace will prove to be enough.

III THE CHRISTIAN'S SETTING

The testing of the sufficiency of grace and peace for daily life comes at this point. For behind the words 'saint' and 'holy' there is the basic idea of 'separation', and when the Christian is entitled a saint he is thereby called to a separate and distinctive life.

Paul teaches us, however, that separation is not segregation, for he addresses those who are 'saints in Christ Jesus *who are at Philippi*'. To be sure they are not of the world, but nevertheless they are in it, and it is in the setting of the life of Philippi that they are to live the distinctive life.

Neither is separation isolation, for Paul writes to '*all* the saints . . . *with* the bishops and deacons'. The church of the apostles was a church with leaders. We must not embark on a discussion of the nature of this leadership beyond what is required in this verse; but this at least is clear, that leadership is not lordship (*cf.* 1 Pet. 5: 3). The preposition is not 'under', nor 'after', but '*with* the bishops and deacons'. The church is a fellowship, and the saint is given this setting also in which to live out his separate, distinctive life.

What then is separation? In a word, it is imitation. 'Be holy, for I am holy' (Lv. 11: 44,45; 19: 2; 20: 26; Mt. 5: 48; 1 Pet. 1: 15; *etc.*). The holiness of God as seen by Isaiah was His moral quality. This is the way of distinctiveness and separation in which the Christian saint is to walk along the streets of Philippi, in the fellowship of believers and the power of a saving Lord.

PHILIPPIANS 1: 3–7

2 ASSURANCE

PAUL'S EXPRESS PURPOSE, as he moves on in his letter from the opening greeting, is to thank God for the fellowship of the saints in Philippi. They have been one with him in gospel work and witness, and he sees this as a gracious act of God for which he is grateful. As we trace out the sequence of thought in these verses, however, we shall discover that, while engaged in thanksgiving, Paul's thoughts find their focus in a great truth, the fact of Christian assurance.

This will become clear if we attempt to summarize the content of the verses. Paul's recollection of the Philippians produces a double fruit; it issues in thanksgiving to God (verse 3), and in joyful intercession on their behalf (verse 4). The particular cause for his thanksgiving is their fellowship in furthering the gospel (verse 5); but all the while, whether engaged in thanksgiving or in supplication, he has an unchanging conviction concerning them (verse 6), that God will never let them go but will make them fully perfect. Now this conviction is a correct one (verse 7), for it is the product of the apostle's love for his friends, and loving them as he does he cannot but feel assured of their permanency in Christ. But, because love is such a 'wishful-thinking' emotion, Paul goes on to ground his convictions about the Philippians on a more solid evidence, namely, that their activity in the defence and proclamation of the gospel is clear proof of a vital partaking of divine grace.

Thanksgiving and supplication (verses 3-5) are grounded upon an abiding conviction (verse 6); this conviction arises out of consideration of evidence (verse 7). In this way it is clear that verse 6 is the pivot upon which the passage turns, and we must therefore make it the first object of our study.

I THE DIVINE BASIS OF ASSURANCE

We shall notice presently how the whole of this small section, verses 3–7, is dominated by the notion of the activity of God. Verse 6 so concentrates upon this notion that no other agent is apparent; God alone is at work.

In the first place, Christian experience was inaugurated by God, 'he . . . began a good work in you'. The verb used is both impressive as to its meaning, and decisive as to the act it describes. According to the commentators, it has solemn, ceremonial connections such as a translation 'to inaugurate' would suggest. Added to this sense of importance in the verb itself, there is the element of decisiveness imparted by the verbal tense used. What was done was not precipitate, nor on a sudden impulse, nor, being well premeditated, did it 'go off at half-cock'. It was planned and executed to perfection.

We can see part of this inauguration of the good work in the case of Lydia, the first of the converts at Philippi. Luke tells us that she gave 'heed to what was said by Paul' (Acts 16: 14), and we may be quite certain that part of his message to Lydia was identical with his later words to the Philippian jailor (16: 31), 'Believe in the Lord Jesus'. And no doubt Lydia could record and recall the very date of her conversion. Nevertheless, when Luke tells her story, it is not cast in terms of placing faith in Christ. His significant phrase is this, 'the Lord opened her heart' (16: 14). It was He who began the good work. But, as we saw in our first study, the opening of the heart was not the real beginning. It was the beginning of conscious experience of the saving grace of God, but the ultimate origin was that solemn enactment of the divine will when He 'chose us in (Christ) before the foundation of the world' (Eph. 1: 4).

Salvation would be a miserably unsure thing had it no other foundation than that I chose Christ. The human will blows hot and blows cold, is firm and unstable by fits and starts; it can offer no security of tenure. But the will of God is the ground of salvation. Sinners would never have been saved had not He so chosen, being moved to do so by His unprovoked and unexplained love (*cf.* Dt. 7: 7,8), and no individual sinner would be saved had he not been made the object of the divine adopting choice before the world was, and had not his heart been opened at the decisive moment to hear the 'word of the truth, the gospel of (his) salvation' (Eph. 1: 13). Herein lies assurance: God has willed my salvation.

God, who thus inaugurated Christian experience, also undertakes for its progress, 'he . . . will bring it to completion'. The translation given by Handley Moule in his *Philippian Studies* is specially instructive, 'will evermore put his finishing touches to it'. The verb is both intensive and continuous. What God began He will persevere with; He will go on perfecting. We will return to this topic again in explaining Philippians 2 : 13, but that must not deter us from dwelling on it here. God never gives up. There is no more dramatic retelling of the story of Israel than Ezekiel 20. The prophet does not spare his people. Their rebellion against God has made their pathway a twisted and devious one. Three times the bell of condemnation rings out: 'But they rebelled' (verses 8,13,21). Four times the bell of assurance rings out: 'I acted for the sake of my name' (verses 9,14,22,44). God would not let His people go. He 'chose Israel' (Ezk. 20: 5) and He will be faithful to that choice until the day comes when 'all the house of Israel, all of them' shall serve God upon His holy mountain (verse 40). He will never give them up, nor go back from His declared will to have this people for Himself. Even so He will go on perfecting us until 'the day of Jesus Christ', and our salvation has this ground of assurance, that its continuance is as certain as the faithful working of the God who cannot lie.

Thirdly, God guarantees the outcome of Christian experience. He began, and He will perfect what He began until 'the day of Jesus Christ'. God is working to a schedule. He is (so to speak) under contract and there is a clause in the contract in which is specified that day and hour which no man knows, not 'even the angels in heaven, nor the Son, but only the Father' (Mk. 13: 32). That day will come for sure, and all will be ready in time for it. There will be no last minute rush, no botching up of the job so as to make it 'do for now'; strikes will not delay it, nor will inefficiency mar it. The Father has beheld the superlative accomplishment of Calvary, and in consequence of this He has bestowed upon His Son the Name above every name (Phil. 2: 9–11), and now nothing will suffice Him but that He will bring His beloved Son out of the invisible glories of heaven and show Him publicly to a wondering and worshipping world, and, to His own glory, see every knee bowed and hear every tongue confessing that Jesus Christ is Lord. And our salvation is as assured as the coming of that day! For it is we, the saints, the believers, the objects of the 'good work' of God, who must be made ready for when He shall come 'on that day to be glorified in his saints, and to be marvelled at in all who have believed' (2 Thes. 1: 10). Here is confidence indeed. Our salvation can no more be forfeited than the Father can break off His pledged purpose to glorify His Son in the day of Christ.

It is surely no wonder, then, that Paul can use the language of a man who has no doubt on the subject. 'I am sure', he says. Looking to the God who begins, continues and ends, he finds no room for uncertainty. This is 'the perseverance of the saints', or better, the perseverance of God with the saints.

II THE HUMAN EVIDENCE OF ASSURANCE

Now it is very clear that when Paul made such a strong and important claim on behalf of the Philippians he was moved to do so by observable facts more than by loving intuition. It was when he recollected their partnership in the gospel (verse 5) that he was led on to express his certainty of their eternal security. Likewise, in verse 7, though the apostle rightly thinks that such love as he feels towards them could only be aroused by Christians as genuine as himself, yet he confesses that he has them in his heart because they are one with him in the defence and confirmation of the gospel. In other words, Christian assurance is the product not only of the truth that God will never forsake His own people or let them slip from His grasp, but also arises from certain observable facts which give immediate evidence that these individuals in particular are true members of the people of God.

This is not, of course, to despise what we may call the inward, and personal, and spiritual aspect of Christian assurance. It is a precious experience to the Christian when 'the Spirit himself (bears) witness with our spirit that we are children of God' (Rom.

8: 16) or when we sense afresh that the love of God is being poured into our hearts by the Spirit (Rom. 5: 5): just as in human relationships there is nothing we prize more than the sense of being loved by those whom we love. Nevertheless, if the professed awareness of being a son of God is not matched by an outward life proper to a son of God, is not the 'awareness' a thin, and possibly an unreal, thing? No New Testament letter is as full of the doctrine of assurance as 1 John, and John in part grounds the assurance of the Christian upon the reality of the indwelling of the Spirit of God (1 Jn. 3: 24; 4: 13). But without question his emphasis rests upon the public testimony of a person's life. There can be no true experience of the love of God if the life gives evidence of lack of compassion (3: 14 ff.). It is keeping His commandments (2: 3; 5: 2), walking as He walked (2: 6) and loving the brethren (3: 14) that give grounds for *knowing* that we are the children of God. Consequently, there is urgent need for the Christian to 'confirm (his) call and election' in the sense in which Peter used those words (2 Pet. 1: 10), seeking as evidence the observable growth of godliness on the basis of faith in Christ.

Paul found such evidence in the Philippians. There are six separate strands of evidence, but they all intertwine around the common theme of the 'gospel'. We may start therefore by noting that Paul discerned between them and himself *unanimity in the truth*: he speaks of their 'partnership in the gospel' (verse 5), and of their work in 'the defence and confirmation of the gospel' (verse 7). He does not need to define what he means by 'the gospel'; he is able to take for granted that they hold to the same good news as he, and which can be summed up in the words 'salvation by faith in Christ': the sermon in one sentence as preached to the Philippian jailor, 'Believe in the Lord Jesus, and you will be saved' (Acts 16: 31). This unanimity of doctrine and of experience is, throughout the New Testament, the sole basis of fellowship. Indeed the word 'partnership' means 'joint-ownership', 'participation in a common object'. The holding of the truth is a mark of the Christian, and a ground of assurance (*cf.* 1 Jn. 4: 13,14).

Paul moves on to mention, secondly, their *concern for the spread of the gospel,* for verse 5 should be translated as in the Revised Version, 'the furtherance of the gospel'. Where there is true possession of the gospel there is also propagation. The gospel is not to be hidden away, but worked with (*cf.* Lk. 19: 11–27). And their evangelistic concern was coupled with the work of *establishing* believers in their faith, described by Paul as the 'confirmation of the gospel'. This word 'confirmation' is related to the word Peter used, in the quotation already made about confirming one's call and election. It occurs again in Hebrews 6: 16 in the expression 'an oath . . . for confirmation', again with the idea of giving something a firmer or more enduring basis, or making it more certain in some respect than it was before. In the present case, therefore, it well expresses the work of edification or strengthening which is the necessary complement to evangelism (*cf.* Acts 14: 22).

The remaining three items may, for brevity, be taken together. Paul saw in the Philippians the feature of *perseverance,* in that they had prolonged their fellowship 'from the first day until now' (verse 5), and *endurance,* in that they were ready to stand for the gospel even when it could involve 'imprisonment' for its adherents, and thirdly, *identification* with the gospel whenever it was called in question, as they leapt to its 'defence' (verse 7). In these three the leading idea is, of course, perseverance. Their association with the gospel was not transient, nor conditional upon favourable circumstances, nor was it silent. They kept on in their faith; they held on to their faith in opposition; they spoke up for their faith when challenged. They persevered. They did not expect people to believe their claim to be the children of God simply because they said so; they showed that it was indeed so. They provided human evidence on which assurance was well based.

III CONFIDENCE AND CAREFULNESS

But though he saw in them evidence for assurance, Paul saw it much more as evidence of grace. When he examined the life of his Philippian friends, and considered their practical devotion to the gospel, he added, 'you are all partakers with me of grace'. It was the grace of God at work in them which produced this fruit.

Really, therefore, Paul's confidence for the Philippians arose from the fact that he saw them as a work of God. In verse 3, he thanks *God* when he thinks of them. Whatever there is of praise-worthiness is to be laid at the door of its divine Author. In verse 6, he views them as begun, continued, and completed by divine workmanship. In verse 7, the fruit of their lives grows out of the partaking of grace. God is at work, and where God works there is certainty of accomplishment.

Paul, however, does not grow complacent. These people, secure as they indeed may be, are yet the objects of his untiring prayer. There is a mystery about prayer which we shall likely never understand. Why does God require it? How, if His will is already determined, does He take it into account? If the Philippians are eternally sure in God, why does Paul need to pray? The questions are neither asked nor answered here, but the apostle clearly shows by his example that, since he has his friends in his heart, the evidence of this will be his prayer for them (*cf.* verses 8,9), and no amount of confidence that God will see them through to the end diminishes his practised carefulness in watching over them by constant supplication, 'as if on that alone hung the issue of the day'. Too often confidence begets complacency, and complacency brings forth prayerlessness. But the apostle, who used language of the greatest emphasis to express his assurance for them—'I am sure'—was equally emphatic about his prayerful concern, 'always . . . every prayer . . . for you all'. The doctrine of assurance, biblically understood, keeps the saint on his toes.

3 GROWING FOR GLORY

AT THE END OF THE PRECEDING STUDY we left Paul at prayer, earnestly concerned for the welfare of his Philippian saints. However, he does not leave the matter there. He is not content to testify to his zeal in prayer; he will also let us know what he is praying and asking for them, and the present verses are taken up with this task.

Like all his recorded prayers, this one is occupied completely with what we must call their spiritual needs. Here he is concerned with their growth, and it is this thought which provides the beginning and ending of his prayer. The key-note is sounded in verse 9, 'abound more and more'. What they are is not enough; there must be increase. In verse 11, the same thought returns in the phrase 'fruit (not fruits) of righteousness'. The abundant increase is to issue in an appointed crop.

I HARVEST-TIME

The picture of the growing Christian which Paul sets before us in the course of his prayer is a strikingly ordered one. As we shall note, there is a growing-point from which the young plant thrusts up two shoots; these bear the blossom which, in turn, yields the fruit. It will aid our study of these things, however, if we look first at the other end, and consider the harvest-time.

The growth of the Christian, says Paul, is 'for the day of Christ', meaning, 'with a view to Christ's coming'. The idea is one of getting ready, being prepared so as to be unashamed (*cf.* 1 Jn. 2: 28). The responsibility for this preparedness is squarely laid upon the Christians by the praying apostle. It is their love which is to abound more and more. It is they who are to advance in knowledge, and to aim at being void of offence when Christ returns.

A truth which recurs in this Epistle must be recognized and faced honestly here. In verse 6 we saw that to prepare for the return of Christ—His day—is the great concern of God Himself, to such an extent that He undertakes the whole work, in its beginning, continuation and end. He will have the Philippians ready for that day. But now, in verses 9–11, Paul sets before these same people a programme of growth and challenges them to get ready. How are these things to be understood? Is it that after all salvation is a co-operative enterprise in which we do our part and God does His? No, that cannot be the case, for salvation is all of God, and the song of the redeemed gathered round the throne in that day will be all occupied with His sole and sufficient grace. It will be entirely 'Glory be to the Father and to the Son and to the Holy Ghost', and not even in the tiniest degree 'Glory be to me'. It will be wholly 'Salvation (belongs) to our God who sits upon the throne, and to the Lamb' (Rev. 7: 10). There will be no glorying of flesh in that day (*cf.* 1 Cor. 1: 26–31). Nevertheless, the word of God to the Christian is always a call to act. He is to 'work' (Phil. 2: 12), run (Phil. 3: 13 f.), and imitate (Phil. 4: 9). He is a soldier, an athlete and a farmer (2 Tim. 2: 3–6). Because he is new-created in Christ there is a programme of good works planned in which he is to serve God (Eph. 2: 10). In other words, it is by his obedience—active, costly, personal, voluntary, disciplined—that the Christian enters into conscious experience of the greatness and fullness of the salvation that is his in Christ.

Such is Paul's view of the Christian in these verses: a man with an objective, a dateline to meet, a Lord to please. He expresses exactly the same thing when he says that the 'fruit of righteousness' (verse 11) is 'to the glory and praise of God'. When Christians are found 'pure and blameless' (verse 10), when they are ready for their returning Lord—this is what brings glory to God and redounds to His praise. God will never be more glorified than when, at the public manifestation of His Son in that day, there will be no discordant note, 'every knee (shall) bow . . . and every tongue confess that Jesus Christ is Lord, *to the glory of*

God the Father' (Phil. 2: 10 f.). And even now there is no greater glory or praise ascribed to God than when believing souls are in readiness for their Lord, that is to say, when they are showing the same concern as is God the Father that the triumph-day of the Saviour will be unblemished. What an objective! How can these things be?

II GROWTH

In preparation for the coming Lord, Paul proposes a programme of growth, and we may, without violence to his teaching, use the metaphor of agriculture, speaking of seed, blade, ear, and full corn, as did our Lord (*cf.* Mk. 4: 26–29). Here is the seed, 'your love' which is to abound, sending forth the blade, 'knowledge and all discernment'. The blade purposes the ear, 'so that you may approve what is excellent', and finally, ready for harvest-time, the full corn, 'and may be pure and blameless'.

Taking these in turn, then, we note first that Paul sees love as the growing-point of the Christian life. It is 'your love' which is to abound more and more. No object of their love is mentioned, and the stress lies on the fact that their own character is to be marked by love, which, presumably, will then reach out to any object, God or man, which presents itself.

It cannot be accidental that before he voiced his prayer that their love might increase Paul had laid the foundation by describing his own love for them, thereby setting an example of what love means to the Christian. He said: 'God is my witness, how I yearn for you all with the affection of Christ Jesus' (verse 8). There was a *reality* in his love for them. It was not just a façade, or a good show put on for the benefit of men, or to keep up an apostolic pretence. He was not afraid to call as Witness God Himself, God who knows the heart. There was also an *intensity* in his love, 'I long after you all.' 'I am homesick for you; I am restless when we are separated.' But the third feature of the apostolic expression of Christian love goes beyond even these two. There was a *quality* in his love for them which made it just such a love as that of Christ Himself: his love was 'with the affection of Christ Jesus'. The Authorized Version, 'in the bowels of', is more literal. It expresses a yearning that is as much physical as mental, a longing love which moves the whole inner being. But what a remarkable expression Paul uses! He loves them 'in the inner being of Christ Jesus'. Certainly this means that he patterns his love for them on that of Christ (*cf.* Eph. 5: 1), but the wording demands something more than the notion of 'imitation'. Paul is saying that he has so advanced in union with Christ that it is as if Christ were expressing His love through Paul. Two hearts are beating as one—indeed one heart, the greater, has taken over and the emotional constitution of Christ Himself has taken possession of His servant.

This third feature of Christian love is, of course, the explanation of the other two. Because he loves them with the love of Christ, it is love that is intense and could not only bear but even invite divine scrutiny. Equally, in this third feature, Paul is indicating the way to true Christian love: by union with Christ, by all that holy and intimate obedience which the Lord Himself described as 'abiding' (Jn. 15 : 1–10). And since the love which he desires to find growing in the Philippians is Christ's own love, we will not be surprised to find it a holy and righteous thing. The antithesis which some make between love and law, between being loving and being righteous, is not found in the Bible, and is explicitly contradicted in this present passage. An attentive reading of verses 9–11 will show either that love is the same thing as righteousness or that love produces righteousness as its fruit. The choice here depends on the meaning of the phrase 'fruit of righteousness' (verse 11). Commentators are divided, and since the two possible meanings are so clear in the phrase the double meaning may have been deliberately left there by Paul.

The first meaning is this: 'the fruit which comes of being right with God'. When a person is 'justified by faith', accounted righteous by God on the ground of faith in Christ, there is envisaged a life of moral fruitfulness to follow. If this is the intended meaning here, then the apostle is seeing the ground of Christian life in two ways. According to verse 9 the basic feature of Christian character is love, and according to verse 11, it is righteousness. Each expresses in its own way the transformation that Christ brings, but the double expression makes a contradiction between love and righteousness impossible.

Alternatively, 'fruit of righteousness' may mean 'a crop of

righteous deeds', and if this is the intended meaning then love is seen as issuing in obedience to the law of God, for there is no other pattern of righteousness available to us (*cf.* Rom. 13: 8–10). Nothing has ever been purer in itself or more productive of pure living than the loving character of the Lord Jesus Christ. The growing Christian commences and continues his progress in holiness by oneness with, and imitation of, his Lord.

As we follow the progress of this harvest theme, we ask in what ways is this seed of love to abound more and more? The answer is unexpected. Love abounds as it puts forth the twin 'blades' of 'knowledge and all discernment'. We would not have immediately associated love and knowledge in this way, but the connection becomes readily understandable if we take a concordance to the word here translated 'knowledge'. It occurs twenty times in the New Testament and always with exclusive reference to knowledge of the things of God, religious knowledge, spiritual knowledge, theological knowledge (*e.g.* Rom. 1: 28, RV; Col. 2: 2). It often carries the idea of seeing into the heart of a matter, grasping what something really is. Thus Paul speaks of the law bringing 'knowledge of sin' (Rom. 3: 20; *cf.* Rom. 10: 2). It is associated with the teaching work of the Holy Spirit, as in Ephesians 1: 17 (*cf.* Col. 1: 9).

But specially instructive for our understanding of this phrase in Philippians are those references which relate 'knowledge' to Christian life and growth. It has four features: (1) This knowledge is the means of salvation, and salvation is described as 'knowledge of the truth' (1 Tim. 2: 4; 2 Tim 2: 25; 3: 7; Heb. 10: 26; *cf.* 2 Pet. 1: 3; 2: 20). (2) Knowledge marks out the Christian as such (Tit. 1: 1; 2 Pet. 1: 2). The Christian is a person 'in the know'. (3) Knowledge is one of the evidences of Christian growth (Col. 1: 10; 2: 2; 3: 10; Phm. 6; 2 Pet. 1: 8). These verses are, of course, very relevant to the present Philippians passage, and a verse like Colossians 2: 2, which associates love and knowledge, is especially so. (4) Knowledge is the state of the full-grown Christian (Eph. 4: 13).

We grow in proportion as we know. Without knowledge of salvation there can be no advancement or progress towards maturity. If we do not know the Lord how can we love Him?

And the more we get to know Him, the more we shall love Him. Consequently, when Paul envisages Christians growing as their love abounds in knowledge, it is not unfair to his thought to say that he sees every Christian as a student. Truth is an essential ingredient in Christian experience. To be a Christian, a man must come to know the truth. To continue and to grow as a Christian a man must increasingly grasp the truth, learning it in depth as well as in breadth. The truth in question here is spiritual knowledge in its widest sense, but in particular the doctrines of salvation. Ignorance is a root cause of stunted growth among Christians. When they fail to live up to the apostolic requirement that they should be equipped 'always . . . to make a defence to any one who calls you to account for the hope that is in you' (1 Pet. 3: 15), they are not only 'letting the side down', they are acting against their own spiritual well-being.

'Every man a Bible student' must be a Christian watchword, and a Christian characteristic. But a great problem still remains. Is it not true that many people seem to increase in knowledge without really growing as Christians, a mental growth unmatched by an increase in character? In order to avoid this danger, we must note that Paul speaks of love abounding in 'knowledge *and all discernment*'. The latter part of his requirement for growth may be well understood by referring to Hebrews 5: 14, where a 'first cousin' of the word 'discernment' is translated 'faculties', 'senses' (RV). By using this word in double-harness with the word 'knowledge' Paul is urging that the Christian student is to concern himself both with finding the truth and with *applying the truth to life*. There is always a double question to be asked when the individual Christian sits before the open Bible: What does it teach? and, How does this truth affect my daily life? Indeed we may confidently say that it is only in connection with these two questions that the Bible would use the word 'knowledge'. 'To know' is not a mere exercise of the head. Nothing is 'known' until it has also passed over into obedience.

The harvest process now naturally proceeds from 'blade' to 'ear', 'so that you may approve what is excellent'. This makes explicit the point just made. As the Christian searches out the truth in the Word of God, and sees its application to life, he has in view the guidance of the whole of his private and public practice by biblical values. He will be faced by many daily choices. For some there will be an unmistakable directive in the Bible, 'The body is not meant for immorality' (1 Cor. 6: 13), for example, or 'Bear one another's burdens' (Gal. 6: 2). But for others there will be no such clear command, and the Christian needs a mind and senses so impregnated with biblical teaching that he will be able to discern and practise the distinctive and superior 'way' that is proper to Christian living. The verb here translated 'approve' has the meanings 'to understand the significance of' (Lk. 12: 56), 'to recognize the quality of' (*e.g.* 1 Cor. 16: 3), 'to approve of' (*e.g.* Rom. 12: 2), and 'to put to the test in practice' (*e.g.* Lk. 14: 19). The word 'what is excellent' (lit., 'the differing things') is used often enough to describe that which is qualitatively superior (*e.g.* Mt. 6: 26; 10: 31), and here may be taken to stand for 'the better course', 'the superior conduct'. The growing Christian is to be marked out by his *recognition* and *practice* of a higher level of life in all situations.

What, in the end, is the 'full corn'? That you 'may be pure and blameless' in readiness for the day of Christ. If the Christian is to be well-pleasing to his returning Lord, the objective is a comprehensive purity of inner and outer life alike. 'Sincerity' (RV) is required as the inner state (*cf.* 2 Pet. 3: 1, of the 'mind'), with the suggestion that not even the all-seeing eye of God can find fault (*cf.* 2 Cor. 1: 12; 2: 17). 'Blameless, void of offence' (RV), whether it means 'without stumbling' or 'causing no offence (to others)', calls for purity of outward life and example. Nothing less than this will do if we are to appear in His presence who of old required of the man who was His friend that he should 'walk before me, and be . . . blameless' (Gn. 17:1).

III POWER

We may well be staggered by such a demand and be so overwhelmed by the hopelessness of the task that we are inhibited from working for its fulfilment. But the harvest metaphor which we have followed throughout will stand us in good stead now. If the seed were capable of feeling anything, doubtless it would despair of ever becoming such a transformed thing as the ear of corn! But the inworking and upsurging life of 'nature' undertakes for all. Equally the Christian, knowing himself as he does, despairs of arriving at that 'fullness' of the 'fruit of righteousness' which is required against the day of Christ. But what are we told here? We are to be 'filled with the fruit of righteousness which come(s) *through Jesus Christ*' (verse 11). A great Agent is at work. The day that is coming is His, and He is the present power, matching the force which, in nature, transforms the seed into the crop.

Does this relegate the Christian to the role of a spectator in the progress of his own sanctification? By no means! The challenge remains, and the objective remains. The individual Christian is responsible for getting himself ready by seeing to it that his love abounds more and more in knowledge and discernment so that he constantly chooses the better path in life and aims at sincerity and constancy. But as he pursues his way he does so in confidence and not in despair, for it is entirely 'through Jesus Christ', and He is sufficient.

4 YESTERDAY, TODAY, AND FOR EVER

WE ARE ALWAYS INTERESTED in the personal circumstances of our friends, and Paul knew that the Philippians were anxiously concerned as to how he was faring. Consequently, having greeted them, and thanked God for them, and having expressed his prayerful hopes for them, the apostle now turns (verses 12–26) to tell them about himself.

To us the verses are no less absorbing than they must have been when first read aloud to the assembled Philippian church. How much we owe to the apostle Paul, and how grateful we are for a window not only into his history but also into his mind such as is provided here! And our motive is more than a loving curiosity, for Paul belonged to that select and never to be repeated apostolic band, the men who could say, as he did on more than one occasion, 'Be imitators of me' (*e.g.* 1 Cor. 11: 1; Phil. 3: 17; 4: 9). There is more here than extracts from the diary of a beloved and fascinating man; there is an example of true Christian living; there is a statement of principle for the guidance of the saints.

In subsequent chapters we will study these verses section by section, but our present purpose is rather to stand back and view the whole. Paul is giving a personal testimony, the verses are full of 'I' and 'me', and as we shall see, one great, overriding truth shines throughout. We must try to grasp this before we attempt to learn from the details of his experiences.

The verses divide themselves out into an ordered statement of the apostle's *past* (verse 12), 'what has happened'; *present* (verses 13–18), 'I am put here' (verse 16), 'I rejoice' (verse 18); and *future* (verses 19–26), 'this will turn out'. We shall divide up our study accordingly.

I THE PAST (*verse 12*)

Paul announces the subject of his remarks, 'what has happened to me'. But even before he does this he has captured our attention by the solemnity, even the urgency, of the opening words of the verse, 'I want you to know, brethren'. It is a feature of Paul's style as a writer to use this, or an equivalent expression, to point to the importance which he attaches to what follows. Here is something not to be glossed over, but a substantial truth calling for close attention (*cf.* Rom. 1: 13; 1 Cor. 10: 1; 11: 3; Col. 2: 1; 1 Thes. 4: 13). It is as if Paul said, 'Now listen carefully to this, because it is something I specially wish you to know and learn.'

It is as well that he arrested our attention, for the remainder of this verse is so well known, and so apparently simple in what it says, that we might easily have passed it by: 'what has happened to me has really served to advance the gospel.' But what a truth is here!

What had in fact happened to Paul? To a certain extent the answer to this question depends on the place from which he was writing this letter, and would therefore require a somewhat technical and involved discussion. The choice is as follows: either Paul was writing from an Ephesian imprisonment, possibly hinted at in verses such as 1 Corinthians 15: 32; or he was imprisoned at Caesarea, as recorded in Acts 24–26; or he was under house-arrest in Rome during the period indicated in Acts 28: 30 f. Those interested in the details of this discussion are referred to the superb treatment of it by Donald Guthrie in the second volume of his *New Testament Introduction* (pp. 92–98 and 144–154). On the whole the Roman hypothesis seems best, and it will also give us the fullest possible view of the great doctrine which Paul is here declaring.

Suppose him, then, imprisoned in Rome. 'What . . . happened' began in Acts 21: 17 when the apostle set foot in Jerusalem, forewarned by the Holy Spirit that bonds and imprisonment awaited him (*cf.* Acts 20:22 f.). Trouble was not long delayed. Though Paul went out of his way to reassure Jewish scruples (21: 26 f.), an entirely false accusation was levelled at him by his own people (21: 28); he was near lynched by a religious mob, and ended up in the Roman prison, having escaped a flogging only by pleading citizenship (22: 22 ff.). His whole case was beset by a mockery of justice, for, though all right was on his side, he could not secure a hearing. He was made the subject of unjust and unprovoked insult and shame (23: 2), malicious misrepresentation (24: 5; 25: 6 f.), and deadly plot (23: 12 ff.; 25: 1 ff.). He was kept imprisoned owing to official craving for popularity (24: 27), or for money (24: 26), or because of an over-punctilious façade of legalism (26: 32). The deceit and malpractice and vilification that surrounded his person were past belief, yet he looks back and asserts that 'what . . . happened to me has really served to advance the gospel'!

Even then his sufferings were not over. There came the prolonged trial of the storm at sea (Acts 27) where his life hung, as it seemed, by a thread, both because of the elements (verse 20) and because of petty officiousness (verse 42). Eventually, when he reached Rome it was far from the ambassadorial entry that he had doubtless looked for (19: 21). He came in the company of the condemned, bound by a chain, and destined to drag out at least two years under arrest awaiting the uncertain decision of an earthly king. Nevertheless, still imprisoned, still chained, still unheard, still uncertain, he looks back and avers, 'what . . . happened to me has really served to advance the gospel'.

Of course, he had enjoyed his moments of relief also. His story was not one of unbroken sadness. He had seen men faithful to him when it was unpopular and even dangerous to be so: the courageous 'son of Paul's sister' (Acts 23: 16), the steadfast Aristarchus (27: 2), the beloved Luke who self-effacingly conceals his welcome presence under the pronoun 'we' (27: 1 ff.); unexpected allies like the centurion, Julius (27: 3,43), unknown ones who cared for him in his need (27: 3) and faced a stained reputation by walking out to meet his sad procession as it neared Rome (28: 15). The Lord Himself was not forgetful either, but stood by in a consciously realized presence at critical moments (23: 11; 27: 23). These also did Paul reckon into his memories when he looked back and said that 'what has happened to me has really served to advance the gospel'.

But notice the word 'really'. It shows in which direction memory is more forcibly leading him. There would be no need to say that the encouragements, human and divine, had tended 'really'—that is to say, contrary to what one might have expected—to advance the gospel's cause. He stresses, therefore, the masses of dark threads that recent years had woven into the fabric of his experience. He says, in so many words, 'Think of the animosities, and bodily pains, the lies, misrepresentations, and deceitfulness, the miscarriage and failure of justice, the agony of being hindered by chains from gospel journeying, and the mental turmoil of appealing to Caesar against my own beloved people (*cf.* Acts 28: 19; Rom. 9: 1–3; 10: 1), the nearness of death and the diminution of hope, the triumph of wickedness and the continued suppression of the truth. Take these things and look them fairly in the face; contrary to what you might have expected, it is *these* things which have fallen out *rather* (RV) to the progress of the gospel.'

One factor has controlled all that has happened to him, and as he looks back he can see it: all has tended to advance the gospel; all has happened under this overruling purpose. But we must ask whether this is a general principle or just a chance happening, or something peculiar to Paul at that one time. Let us assert at once the greatness of what Paul is here illustrating by his own experience. This is not a truth peculiar to apostles, nor something that is occasionally true, nor something that is to be asserted as true when it is clearly seen in experience to be so. *It is always true,* because Christian life as such is lived out under the conviction that 'he who began a good work in you will keep on bringing it to perfection until the day of Jesus Christ' (see verse 6). It is God who rules. The pressures of life are the hands of the Potter who is also our Father (Is. 64: 8). The fires of life are those of the Refiner (Mal. 3: 3). He will no more abandon this perfecting process to others, or to chance, than He will abandon His purpose to vindicate and glorify His own Son in the crowning day. This God is too great to be knocked off course by the malpractice of wicked men or by the inactivity of good but weak men. For 'God is not man, that he should lie, or a son of man, that he should repent. Has he said, and will he not do it? Or has he spoken, and will he not fulfil it?' (Nu. 23: 19).

II THE PRESENT (*verses 13–18*)

Paul did not leave his problems behind when the door of his house-prison closed behind him. When he reviews his present circumstances for the benefit of the Philippians and us, he reveals a situation of real personal vexation. It is most noticeable how he avoids dwelling on the personal inconvenience of his bonds, though it takes little imagination to feel the tugging chain whenever he moved, even if he did no more than reach for a drink of water, or the tiresomeness of never being alone but always under surveillance. Yet these things are not elaborated. Paul directs the gaze of his readers elsewhere, into the Christian world in which he is placed. There is a group on each side, and he between them. The one is composed of those who are unfeignedly his friends, acting out of goodwill and love for the apostle and his cause; the others are moved by some sort of spleen against him. It is not a situation he can ignore, for he has been thrust into it willy-nilly by those who have made him explicitly the target of their attack, not to mention that he is the head of the church and therefore must take some form of line. What is he to choose? Will he excommunicate these people because of their attitude towards him, and the unfavourable atmosphere which they doubtless created, or will he ignore them altogether?

Paul does not make himself neutral in all this, nor does he take a merely negative attitude. He has a positive and clear approach to the problems of the present. He states it in verse 18, 'What then? Only that in every way, whether in pretence or in truth, Christ is proclaimed; and in that I rejoice. Yes, and I shall rejoice.' 'Christ is proclaimed'—not just 'Christ is unoffended or uninvolved'. How often Christians justify a course of action on the ground of an uninvolved Christ! How often we feel that we may do this or that, engage in this or that, simply because 'it does not hinder me as a Christian' or 'it has no bearing on Christian living one way or the other'! Paul was more positive: is Christ *preached*? Does this clearly give a testimony to Him? If he moves in this way or in that will it promote the declaration of Christ, the cause of the gospel?

When he offers this as his criterion in making present decisions, he is, of course, setting us an example. This positive test of whether or not 'Christ is proclaimed' would decide many issues for us, and would lead us from much unprofitable, even if harmless, expenditure of time into more fruitful paths. But what, in a word, is he saying? That the principle which, according to verse 6, he sees as governing all history, and which, according to verse 12, has governed his own immediate past, must also be put to work to govern present decisions and actions. God bends His divine government of His people towards the day of Christ's glory. Paul discerns that events are turned to 'advance the gospel' and he makes his daily choices according to what he perceives will best and most 'proclaim Christ'. There is no difference, though it is stated in different ways. One factor runs through all —Christ and His glory.

III THE FUTURE (*verses 19–26*)

The same great governing interest holds good when the apostle turns to consider the future. He is faced by the same broad possibilities we all face: he will either die or live. He may be uncertain, as all are, of the detailed circumstances surrounding these possibilities, but the possibilities themselves are unmistakable. What principle guides him as he walks forward into the coming days? He gives a magnificent answer: 'now as always Christ will be honoured in my body, whether by life or by death' (verse 20). There is no 'wait and see' about Paul. As we shall observe in greater detail in a later study, Paul does not adopt a 'know-all' attitude towards the future. He does not know whether it is his lot to die at once or to live on. Faced with the choice, he hardly knows what he will choose. The future is unknown and to the eye of man, even of a man such as Paul, uncharted. But his mind is made up on one thing: let the future bring what it will, 'Christ will be honoured in my body, whether by life or by death.' There is no uncertainty on this score. He sees his coming task, in whatever manner he must discharge it, to be in essence this: not to carry a snapshot of Christ in his wallet for occasional showing to chosen folk, but to show an enlarged, life-size Christ to all who care to look, a Christ fully displayed in every dimension and capacity of Paul, a Christ 'magnified in his body' (RV).

Christ is thus the central and controlling factor for Paul, and for all who would live in the apostolic mould. All things are organized, whether we can see it or not, so as to tend towards preparedness for the day of Christ. He is the key of all history and of personal history. He is to be the deciding factor in every Christian choice. Pre-eminence must be given to that which is judged to advance the gospel and to proclaim the Saviour. He is the object of the Christian's supreme resolve as he faces the future and makes the glory of Christ his great, controlling interest. 'In the soup' of circumstances, past, present, and future, the Christian is a person who 'sees no man, save Jesus only'.

5 SUFFERING

WE HAVE NOW TAKEN A BIRD'S-EYE VIEW of this great passage (1: 12–26) and we have seen the single principle of the glory of Christ which runs throughout. In the course of his review, however, the apostle displays himself in three typical situations: faced by personal suffering (verses 13,14), a divided church (verses 15–18), and an uncertain future (verses 19–26). Before we go on we must glance at his example and teaching under each of these three headings.

The linking thought in verses 13 and 14 is the expression 'my imprisonment', or 'my bonds' (RV). In this undramatic way Paul calls attention to himself as a sufferer. We have already noticed that he does not elaborate his discomforts so as to call attention to himself: that would be unseemly in a man professing to subdue his body to the greater consideration of the glory of Christ. He does not, therefore, concentrate our gaze on the chained wrist, but, as it were, holding up the chain before our eyes, he makes us look through its links at the effect of these 'bonds' upon the world and the church.

1 THE FRUITFULNESS OF CHRISTIAN SUFFERING

Refusing the way of self-pity, Paul does not describe the effect of the bonds upon himself, then, but their effect upon others. And first, he tells us that his bonds were a testimony to the world. Indeed, it is this which helps him to his great conclusion that the things which happened to him had served to advance the gospel. The gospel progressed in this way, it became 'known throughout the whole praetorian guard and to all the rest that my imprisonment is for Christ', or RV, 'my bonds became manifest in Christ'.

The praetorian guard was a picked division of crack imperial troops. Membership of this regiment was much sought after, since double pay and special conditions of service were enjoyed, and there were good pension prospects as well as special duties. We gather from the reference here that one of the duties was to mount guard over prisoners awaiting trial before the Caesar himself, and we can imagine a long line of praetorians who took it in turn to be Paul's warders. No doubt the apostle to the Gentiles was not slow to tell them of the Lord Jesus Christ, and, apart from such testimony, they were the witnesses of many sessions between Paul and those who freely visited his house (Acts 28: 30 f.), so that the gospel had advanced among the praetorian guard, and also amongst 'all the rest', making a general impact upon the Roman public. But when asked to say how this impact was made he holds up his chains, 'my bonds became manifest' (RV). It was precisely his suffering that was fruitful in making a testimony to the world.

His bonds had a second effect: they were a stimulus to the church. Christians were stirred up to bolder and more effective preaching. This fourteenth verse is very instructive on the subject of Christian testimony. First, we learn who are the *agents* in witness, 'the brethren'. The modern church, sadly, would be more inclined to say that testimony is the work of 'bishops and deacons' (verse 1), those set apart for 'full-time' service. They are the mouthpiece of the church to the world. It was not so in the apostolic church, and it was something quite other than this relegation of responsibility which gladdened the imprisoned Paul. 'The brethren' were out on the job telling the world of Christ. Needless to say this teaching prevails through the New Testament, and, indeed, Paul returns to it in Philippians 2: 15 f. where it is the individual Christian, the man or woman who can speak of his 'own salvation' (2: 12), who is to be seen as a 'light in the world, holding forth the word of life' (RV). Here, incidental to his example of Christian suffering, is a piece of apostolic teaching on the nature of ministry and service in the church to which we must, for our very life's sake, return in the present day. The world has already seen what can happen when one man is wholly given to the Lord and absorbed in telling of Him; that man was Paul. But the world has yet to see a whole church on the march, a people of God on fire for God. Something like this began to mark the church of Rome during Paul's imprisonment; it is surely the will of God that His people should be wholly mobilized for service.

Paul tells us also of the *power* which marked their service and where it originated. They were 'confident in the Lord'. While Paul was a bound prisoner, Christians were somehow being led to take a firmer and more confident grip upon Christ; they began to be less timid; Christ was freshly seen as trustworthy and they trusted Him.

This became evident in the *manner* of their witness, which was 'much more bold . . . without fear'. This is remarkable. They saw before their very eyes, in Paul himself, what could happen when a man waxed bold for Christ. Was not this why he was in prison, chained, distressed in body? Was not his zeal for Christ the cause of his arrest and the subject of his impending trial, and, likely enough, the charge for which the death penalty would be exacted? Yet they suddenly lost fear, and the instinct for self-preservation began to wither, and a new boldness and fearlessness took charge of them.

The *substance* of their witness follows in sequence from the two points just made. Their power derived from the Lord, and their boldness naturally followed. What else, then, could they talk of but Him? They spoke 'the word of God'. But Paul comes to grips more precisely with their topic. The 'word of God' of verse 14 is defined in verse 15 as 'some indeed preach Christ' and in verse 17 as 'the former proclaim Christ' and in verse 18 as 'Christ is proclaimed'. Their message was not self-originated, but derived from God in His word; their message was not self-advertising but a proclamation (verse 15, 'preach' means 'herald') and a forth-telling (verses 17,18) of Christ.

The church was stimulated into gospel-action. But the point of stimulation was the suffering of the apostle. The brethren were 'confident in the Lord because of my imprisonment'. Here again is the fruitfulness of Christian suffering. The imprisoned, suffering Paul was not 'on the shelf', out of action. His great work still went forward along the twin lines of testifying to the world and stimulating the church. His suffering was a positive, fruitbearing thing.

II THE EXPLANATION OF THE FRUITFULNESS

Not every suffering Christian is as fruitful as was the apostle, nor even fruitful in any sense at all. Many a Christian suffers without exercising any influence for good upon the world or the church. In other words, the fruitfulness, though it stemmed from Paul's suffering—his 'imprisonment', his 'bonds'—is not explained by it. There must be some other explanation.

Four truths, all about Paul the sufferer, encircle the fact of his suffering. The first we have already observed but must now return to it again in its proper place: in his suffering he was *self-effacing*. He did not use the occasion of suffering either to turn his thoughts in upon himself or to make himself the object of other people's attention and interest. These verses (13,14), with their common foundation in the words 'my imprisonment', are as outward-looking as any pair of verses in the New Testament. He makes us look at the bonds, not at the wrists which they chafed and bruised; and he makes us look at the bonds only so that we may better appraise the impact they made upon the world and the church.

Secondly, Paul the sufferer was still *witnessing* to Christ. He writes that 'it has become known . . . that my imprisonment is for Christ'. How did it become known? One chained man looks much the same as another. The manacles tell nothing, but the man does. Here was a prisoner whose talk was all of Another. Whether he sat alone with his guard, or whether a visitor called, the talk was always the same; it was all Christ. The suffering was the occasion of testimony to the Lord.

The verbal testimony was rooted in Paul's inner attitude towards his suffering. He saw himself—chain and all!—as a man *under orders*. He writes, 'I am put here for the defence of the gospel' (verse 16; AV, verse 17). The term used here is military. When the time came that a praetorian's period of guard duty was over, he was relieved by another. The chain was passed from hand to hand and the new guard was 'set' to keep watch over Paul. It was not his part to query the duty allotted to him: such decisions were made by other minds in other places. However he might have planned his service to lie in other and more exciting, and apparently more worth-while, enterprises, this was what was required of him, and this was the situation in which to uphold the traditions of the regiment to which he belonged and to win his superior's praise. But Paul was just as much 'on duty' as he was! Perhaps we may venture to imagine what went through the apostle's mind when a sentry entered for the first time. 'He has come in here because he is on duty; he is "set" to guard me. Wouldn't he be surprised to learn that I am every bit as much on duty as he is, that I am "set" to guard him for Christ!' Paul did not see his suffering as due to divine forgetfulness ('Why did God allow this to happen to me?'), nor as a dismissal from service ('I was looking forward to years of usefulness, but here I am chained to the house'), nor as the work of Satan ('I am afraid the devil has had his way this time'), but as the place of duty, the appointed setting of service, the work at present required. The great ambassador of Christ is not free to bear the tidings of the Lord over land and sea as before, but he has not ceased to be an ambassador. The form of the ambassadorship has changed but the purpose and duty of it still remains—'an ambassador in chains' (Eph. 6: 20).

All this is summed up in saying that in and through his suffering Paul was utterly *dedicated* to Christ. Shortly, as he looks into the future, he will use words which express his present and abiding mood, '*now* as always Christ will be honoured in my body' (verse 20). How those words '*now* as always' need to eat their way into heart and mind and conscience alike! For all of us each passing moment is a unique thing, unlike anything else, unrepeatable. It is now, now, now, that we must show how great Christ is. Never again will we have the chance to live for Him through *this* moment; never again will we have the chance to please Him in *this* circumstance; never again will He be gladdened by the trust in Him which we have shown in the face of *this* test. It elates the heart to write these words, and the spirit rises to dedicate itself in love to Christ. But there was small elation for Paul as he looked at his chain, and his flesh worn by its constant chafing, and felt his muscles ache with its dragging weight. No elation, but as he looked he resolved, '*now* as always'.

6 DIVISIONS

AS PAUL VIEWED THE ROMAN SCENE from the vantage-point of his hired house, it was not wholly to his liking. In verse 14 we sense Paul's delight in the forward move of the gospel through the ministry of an awakened church, but verses 15–18 open other windows into the state of affairs, and we learn that all was not quite so rosy.

The first of the disquieting facts to notice is that Paul observes men whose hearts were at war with their testimony. The preachers at work in the Roman church were of two sorts, differentiated by their attitude towards the apostle. The one group consisted of those who felt unfeigned goodwill towards him, and all their Christian activity was motivated by love for him, springing out of their knowledge that he was 'put (there) for the defence of the gospel' (verse 16). On the other side stood those who worked in order to 'afflict me in my imprisonment' (verse 17).

We are not permitted to take the easy way out in this distinction, and to say that the one group was Christian in name and and in reality while the other was Christian in name only, or even heretical. Some commentators have, indeed, taken this line, urging that we have here some sort of sect, or break-away group, possibly those called 'Judaizers', or 'Christ-plus' men, who added requirements like circumcision or other Mosaic precepts as essential for salvation (see Acts 15: 1,5; contrast Acts 15: 8,9,11). But it seems certain that whoever these men were, they cannot have been Judaizers, for there is nothing here of the extreme sternness of language which Paul felt obliged to use when he proclaimed an anathema upon such troublers of the church (Gal. 1: 6–9), or did not hesitate to call them 'dogs' (Phil. 3: 2). On the contrary, he extends complete approval to the message these men preached, 'Christ is proclaimed' (verse 18), and Paul felt nothing but joy in the fact.

They were Christian preachers, then, but divided men. And not just divided from other Christians, but divided internally; their hearts were at war with their testimony. For even while they preached Christ they nourished emotions inimical to the gospel.

Paul tells us of their 'envy' (verse 15). What were they envious of? He does not say. He is as reticent here about the sins of others as he was in verses 13 and 14 about his own sufferings. The details are not filled in. It may have been that they envied the great gifts which God had given the apostle, for sometimes men cannot tolerate that others should be more highly endowed than they. It may be that they envied the great success that had hitherto attended Paul's ministry. It may be that they envied and resented the way in which he became automatically the focus of Christianity in Rome—that their noses were put out of joint by his arrival. We might go on guessing, and any or all of our surmises might well be the case. Paul does not tittle-tattle about the sins of others. He says 'envy' and leaves it there.

There was also 'rivalry' (verse 15), and 'partisanship' (verse 17). They were moved by a sheer desire to oppose others (rivalry) and to fight for themselves (partisanship). While everybody else was wrong, they were wholly right! There are the two abiding facets of sectarianism, or the worst aspects of denominationalism.

Finally, Paul invades the realm of motive explicitly: they preach 'not sincerely', that is to say, with mixed motives, for alongside the great motive for preaching, the glory of Christ in the conversion of sinners and the edification of saints, there was this other, 'thinking to afflict me in my imprisonment'. Observe again the reticence of the apostle. 'If any one thinks he is religious, and does not bridle his tongue but deceives his heart, this man's religion is vain' (Jas. 1: 26). How magnificently Paul here passes this stern test! There is complete absence not only of a retaliatory spirit, but also of a liberated tongue. Did Paul not feel the hurt they inflicted? Of course he did—he who knew the inexpressible sadness of 'danger from false brethren' (2 Cor. 11: 26); but he does not dwell on what they did to him, and to this day we do not know.

All we know is that they committed the cardinal sin of the preacher, to use his pulpit to make sly innuendoes and veiled attacks and concealed, damaging hints against someone else. And they exposed themselves to the danger of spiritual schizophrenia, the attempt to hold two positions at once. On the one hand they were apparently faithful gospel preachers, committed to declare a selfless, self-sacrificing, unself-seeking Christ, a Christ bent upon the eternal good of all whom He died to save. On the other hand they privately and secretly indulged a different set of values, self-seeking, self-regarding, moved by desire to hurt one whom Christ had died to save. They were double-minded, dual personalities. Their public lives warred with their private lives, and their tongues with their thoughts.

The Bible is very emphatic in its warnings of the spiritual peril of such a double life, not least, for example, when Proverbs (4: 23) counsels to 'keep your heart with all vigilance; for from it flow the springs of life', or when Paul orders the Romans to cast off not only the bodily sins of 'revelling and drunkenness . . . debauchery and licentiousness' but also the sins of the spirit, 'quarrelling and jealousy', and those of the mind when he says 'and take no forethought (make no provision) for the flesh' (Rom. 13: 12–14). Indeed, in the present Epistle he emphatically calls the Philippians to cultivate the opposite virtues to those described here: 'the same love, being in full accord', doing 'nothing from selfishness or conceit' (Phil. 2: 2 f.). But in the present passage he does not even pause to issue warnings. He is describing what he finds, and in so far as he has a purpose in his description it is not to denounce the divided loyalties of his opponents, nor their deceitfulness, nor to point them to a remedy. His purpose rather is to show how a Christian ought to behave when faced with a divided *church*, what things may be ignored, what deserves priority, to what principle an appeal may be made, and what is to be left out of account.

We must move on, then, with the apostle. Later verses will raise again the topic of divided loyalties and the bearing of vices like faction and self-seeking upon the constitution and witness of the church, but at the moment we must look through the apostle's eyes at what is a very familiar situation today.

The church was divided within itself. There were the Paulinists (verse 15) and the anti-Paulinists (verse 17). We must notice again the absence of detail in Paul's description. We do not in fact know how either side behaved. There is nothing in these verses which limits their application to a local situation of long ago. This may, of course, have been Paul's purpose in leaving so much detail unsaid. At any rate, the result of his silence is that we have a passage which raises great and permanent Christian issues in their simplest form, and lays down an equally great and simple approach to them.

Local and world-wide divisions in the church are one of the features of our day. To mention again the list of sins which Paul gave in Romans (13: 13), it is likely enough that no local church in this country is greatly bothered by revelling and drunkenness, debauchery and licentiousness; it is equally likely that most local churches are harbouring quarrelling and jealousy! There is always this sort of division among Christians somewhere. Of the more public and publicized denominational divisions which sunder the visible church, we need not speak in detail: they are all too obvious. Now it is not being naïve to say that Paul here sees in miniature, in one church or local situation, exactly what faces us today both locally, and nationally, and internationally: two sets of people, both claiming the name of Christian, but not at one, not easy with each other, divided.

A few negative statements will clear the ground for the great positive principle which Paul enunciates for dealing with this state of affairs. First, he does not deal with the problem of division by means of the doctrine of sanctification. There were clear spiritual defects in the one party, but the apostle does not say or even hint that if only they were better Christians, more sanctified, more Christlike, the divisions would speedily disappear and all cause for disaffection would be gone. This of course is true. If all Christians were completely Christlike there would be no divisions. Nevertheless, this is not a present solution to the problem, and Paul ignores it. The reason, of course, is obvious: such sanctification will come only with the return of Christ, when we shall see Him and be like Him (1 Jn. 3: 2). No doubt Paul would have been honest enough to admit that in some of the respects in which they disliked him he merited their dislike. He had not 'already obtained' neither was he 'already perfect' (3: 12). No doubt those who loved him were not themselves altogether lovely or lovable. Unity among Christians, and the healing of divisions, has to be achieved *in spite of* imperfect sanctification, and to make unity depend on holiness is, at this stage of the divine economy for the church, crying for the moon.

More surprisingly, Paul does not deal with the problem of unity by means of the doctrine of apostolicity. 'He is apparently quite unconscious of the thought that because he is the one apostle in Rome grace can be conveyed only through him, that his authority and commission are necessary to authenticate teaching and to make ordinances effectual' (Moule, *PS*). This narrow conception of apostolicity as centring in the apostolic person truly seems to be beyond Paul's horizon of interest and teaching. The argument from silence here is thoroughly supported by such a document as 2 Timothy, where, envisaging Timothy throughout as living in a divided church (1: 15 f.; 2: 17 f.; 3: 1–5; 4: 3 f.), he not once suggests that Timothy in his own person as apostolic delegate (and undoubted recipient of the laying on of apostolic hands, see 1: 6) is the focus of unity and the only allowable safeguard of the unity and purity of the church, alike in doctrine and practice. This view of apostolicity, so tragically and damagingly prevalent today, finds no place, echo, nor encouragement in Paul, and his attitude towards the divisions at Rome is a case in point.

Even more surprisingly, neither does he solve the problem of divisions by appealing to the centrality of the Person of Christ. He does not say in a bland and sweeping way that since we all follow the one Lord we are all one. His emphasis is not upon the *Person* of Christ, but upon the *proclamation* of Christ. We may return to the quotation from Bishop Moule which we commenced above: 'Paul would far rather have order, and he knows he is its lawful centre. But the announcement of Christ is a thing even more momentous than order. . . . If even a separatist propaganda will extend the knowledge of *Him,* His servant can rejoice. . . . Surely even in our day, with its immemorial complications of the question of exterior order, it will tend more than anything else to straighten crooked places . . . if we look, from every side, on the glory of the blessed Name, as our supreme and ruling interest.'

Now this is not simply saying that 'we can at least evangelize together' and sink our differences in a common concern for the lost. The exactness of what Paul said, and insisted upon, must be noticed. Paul's experiences have fallen out 'to advance the gospel' (verse 12) with this result that the brethren speak 'the word of God' with boldness (verse 14), and 'preach Christ' (verse 15), and 'proclaim Christ' (verse 17), so that in and through it all 'Christ is proclaimed' (verse 18). Paul is here giving the weight of his authority and approval *not* to their devotion to Christ as such, *nor* to their concern for the unconverted as such, but to the fact that he agrees with and authenticates *their message*.

Differences of personal like and dislike must ever remain in the church. Different stages of sanctification must ever mark individual Christians and groups of Christians on this side of glory. These things must be accepted, and, as far as unity is concerned, set on one side. There is but one essential. In its broadest statement, it is agreement in the truth; in its inner essence, it is agreement as to what constitutes the saving message, the gospel, what we tell the world about Christ. Lacking this we will look in vain for unity; having it we have the one thing on which Paul here insists, and which remains the single point of insistence throughout the New Testament teaching on the unity of the church.

7 LOOKING FORWARD

AS WE SAW IN OUR OUTLINE of this section of the Epistle, Paul follows his review of past events (verse 12), and his account of present circumstances (verses 13–18), by an attempt to peer forward into the future (verses 19–26). In studying this latter division more closely, we find Paul characterized by *certainty*, and *uncertainty*. He is quite sure about some things: he says 'I know' (verse 19), and 'my eager expectation and hope' (verse 20, recalling that the New Testament use of the word 'hope' is full of confidence and contains nothing of the unsureness which modern usage has imported into it). Equally, in some things he is uncertain, saying 'which I shall choose I cannot tell' (verse 22). Examination will show that his certainty belongs to the realm of *ambition*: he knows what he is out for; uncertainty belongs to the realm of detailed out-working: he is not sure just how things will shape out.

I THE CHRISTIAN'S AMBITION (*verses 19,20*)

Paul opens up his attitude towards the future by speaking of his 'salvation' (verse 19, RV). By translating this word as 'deliverance', RSV narrows its reference so that it points only to the ending of the apostle's imprisonment. There is great value, however, and indeed, greater accuracy in context in the translation 'salvation'. The word 'salvation' and the verb 'to be saved' have a threefold reference, as a glance through a concordance will show. They look back to the past, as Paul does when he reminds the Ephesians how they 'heard the word of the truth, the gospel of your salvation' (Eph. 1: 13). Henceforward, many Christians at Ephesus could look back and say: 'On such and such a day I was saved.' And Paul reflects this 'dated' aspect of salvation when he says, 'By grace you have been saved' (Eph. 2 : 8). Now the AV of that verse gives a present tense, 'By grace are ye saved', and this is also correct, for the Greek verb, strictly understood, tells of a past fact which has continued into the present and is still true. Consequently, salvation is a present experience also, and it is in this light that Paul commands the Philippians to 'work out' their own salvation (2 : 12). It is something they possess, but they are to enter into fuller and fuller present realization of its richness and greatness. This process of increasing present enjoyment of salvation has an end: the possession of salvation in its completeness, to which Paul looks forward when he says that 'salvation is nearer to us now than when we first believed' (Rom. 13: 11).

It is in this third sense that Paul uses 'salvation' here: he is envisaging his personal full enjoyment in the day of Christ of that which he partly and progressively enjoys here and now (*cf.* 3: 13 f.). It is his ambition to get there! Three distinct things promote the attaining of this future salvation.

a. The outworking of events

'For I know', he says, 'that this shall turn to my salvation' (verse 19, RV). 'This' refers to the situation in which he finds himself placed as he writes: the Roman church, divided though it is, stimulated into vigorous and fearless preaching through Paul's bondage among them. Back behind 'this' lies the long series, chiefly of misfortunes, which we summarized earlier. It will 'turn to my salvation'; it will 'issue in' my personal experience of the fullness of everything which Christ accomplished for me at Calvary.

In so many ways, the longer we study Philippians, the more we find ourselves led time and again to the basic truth so clearly taught in 1 : 6, 'He who began a good work in you will bring it to completion at the day of Jesus Christ.' Paul is saying exactly that all over again when he asserts that 'this shall turn to my salvation'. He expresses his personal confidence, and urges it upon us as a sure faith for ourselves also, that the Christian need never fear the outcome of events. Life brings (as we say) its daily pressures; many of them are unexpected; some of them are unpleasant; often they seem uncalled-for; from time to time they are traceable to the malignity of wicked men (and there is no doctrine of divine sovereignty which relieves such men of a heavy guilt in the matter; the doctrine of sovereignty rather guarantees their punishment, *cf.* Acts 2 : 23). But God is over all, and there is no point in believing in a sovereign God if He can be tumbled off the throne by human or satanic agency! Philippians 1: 6 tells us about this God, beginning, completing, and purposing to finish His good work in and for us. Romans 8: 28 tells us about our personal history in which 'in everything God works for good'. Paul takes and accepts this great and comfortable truth in a precise and unpleasant period of his life, 'This shall turn to my salvation.'

b. The prayers of other Christians

The Christian, however, is not a cork on the waters, carried along by the tide of circumstances. He is a person in need of help from God if he is to sustain the pressures of life and live for Christ through them. Such help is there for him. Paul calls it 'the help (RV, 'supply') of the Spirit of Jesus Christ' (verse 19). 'Supply' has a 'plus' element in it; it is the 'full, sufficient supply'. 'Of the Spirit' means either that the Spirit is the Bearer of the full supply to us, in His great office of making real in our experience all the benefits and blessings of faith in God (*cf., e.g.,* Rom. 8: 11), or else that the Spirit Himself is the full supply as He indwells the believer. He is called the 'Spirit of Jesus Christ' because His presence in us and His gracious work for us have been purchased by the saving work of Christ (*e.g.* Jn. 7: 39; Acts 2 : 33; Gal. 4 : 4–6). Thus, God not only rules our lives from the throne, but He also sustains our lives from within.

This, however, is in answer to the prayers of other Christians. The two thoughts of intercession and supply are bound so closely together by Paul that we could, without violence, translate the Greek, 'your prayers and the consequent supply. . . .' Paul could have asked for the Spirit for himself, and no doubt often did. It is a God-given privilege to ask for the Holy Spirit, and each is invited to do so (Lk. 11 : 13). But Paul turned the matter in another direction: he displayed himself as concerned for the spiritual welfare of the Philippians, and his love for them issued in prayer (1: 4,8,9). He also needs and asks for their prayers. This is our mutual responsibility and interdependence: a common and reciprocal obligation to put each other's spiritual growth in the very forefront of our supplication, and to take the responsibility as seriously as to say even this (which Paul very sensitively suggests), that the sufficient supply of the Spirit of Jesus Christ for my brother or sister in Christ depends directly on my prayer for them, and that failing my prayer the supply will dry up also.

c. The Christian's personal efforts

In the third place Paul comes to his own responsibility in this matter of final salvation. God will bring him there; the prayers of Christians will sustain him on his way; meanwhile he himself is a person of absorption, confidence, and determination in the pursuit of a great ambition. Without, at the moment, dwelling on the significance of this in relation to the doctrine of sanctification, it will be better to see the emphasis which Paul here lays upon these three elements in his make-up.

His *absorption* is expressed in the word 'eager expectation'. The single Greek word here has three elements in it, 'away', 'the head' and 'to watch', and these are combined to give the idea of 'watching something with the head turned away from other objects'. Paul's attention is wholly occupied with one thing, to the exclusion of others. This is essentially the same picture as he gives when he sees himself as a runner (3: 13 f.) expending every effort as he speeds to the tape. This absorption is founded on *confidence*; 'eager expectation' rests upon 'hope', which in the New Testament means something whose coming is certain, but whose timing is uncertain. He does not tell us now the ground of this certain hope, for he has already made it plain. What can it be but that he has a like confidence in God for himself as for the Philippians, that God will see him safely home (1: 6), and that Christ will prove sufficient for every eventuality on the road (1: 11)?

The exertions of a Christian man are not the doomed efforts of the unregenerate to merit glory, but are the expressions of that new life in Christ which he already possesses and the appointed means whereby he experiences more fully the greatness of his possession.

The *determination* with which Paul pursues his goal moves along three lines. First, inwardly, there is determination to preserve a clear conscience—'that I shall not be at all ashamed' (*cf.* Acts 24: 16); second, outwardly, determination to maintain a bold testimony—'but that with full courage', a word which primarily refers to unreservedness and absence of concealment in speech (*cf.* Eph. 6: 19); third, upwardly, determination to keep an unblemished record—'now as always'.

With what is Paul absorbed? To what end does he feel confidently that he will be upheld? On what is the determination of conscience, tongue, and life concentrated? Here is the Christian's ambition as he faces an otherwise unknown future, 'Christ will be honoured in my body, whether by life or by death.' This is what God is doing (1: 6) as He purposes to make the saints ready for the great day; it is what God is doing as He rules and overrules in the circumstances of His people (1: 12,19); and it is what He expects His people to do by the conscious, constant, and demanding effort of the daily consecration of conscience and will to the life of obedience.

II THE CHRISTIAN'S INDECISION (*verses 21–26*)

The Christian's hope makes the outcome certain, but leaves both the time and the means in question. Thus, at the end of verse 20 Paul can only express alternative possibilities, 'life . . . or . . . death'. In this regard he does not know what the future contains, except that it must be either the one or the other. We will attempt to follow the course of his thought under three headings.

a. The equal desirability of life and death (verses 21,22)

What does Paul mean when he says that for him 'to live is Christ, and to die is gain'? A later passage in the Epistle must be allowed to interpret this one. In 3: 7 f. Paul reveals the things which make life meaningful for him, and uses the word 'gain' in a way which we must take as a definition of what he means by it. Looking back to his past, he recalls lovingly the day when Christ became everything to him (3: 7). He candidly added up all that he had previously counted valuable (the list given in 3: 4–6) and he found Christ to possess a superior worth, and gladly surrendered all to and for Him. But this attitude persists, and Paul turns to a present tense (3: 8): he is still 'counting' and still finding the surpassing worth of Christ, so that his whole life may be summed up as the progressive abandonment of everything else in the interest of possessing more and more of Christ.

'Gaining Christ', then, is another way of expressing the Christian's progressive experience of sanctification, growth in grace, or approximation more and more to the likeness of Jesus. Returning to 1: 21, Paul defines his life as a gaining of Christ, and death as the ultimate gain itself. In life he is absorbed and determined in consecrated living for Christ; in death he expects to enter upon a total possession. We could paraphrase and extend his thought by saying, 'Life means Christ to me, Christ more and more fully known and loved and served as day follows day; death means Christ to me, Christ once for all and finally possessed and eternally enjoyed.'

What then is he to choose? He confesses, 'I am hard pressed between the two' (verse 23)! The benefits, as he sees them, are evenly balanced, for against the immediate gain of Christ which death brings, he finds he must take into account the increased fruit for Christ which continued life will bring (verse 22). This seems to be the broad meaning of verse 22, though the Greek is difficult, and the commentaries should be consulted as to the variety of possible shades of meaning. We, however, will offer one opinion only. In language that is somewhat broken because of the intensity of feeling on these matters, Paul begins to discuss in verses 22 and 23 the alternative courses stated in verse 21. 'To live is Christ' (verse 21); very well, then 'if (my lot is) to be life in the flesh, that means fruitful labour for me. (Then) which I shall choose I cannot tell.' Death is a glorious possession of Christ; life is a glorious bearing of fruit! He finds the choice pulls him in two.

b. The preference for death (verse 23)

Faced with this double possibility, Paul attempts some assessment of what is involved in each course, and confesses here (verse 23) that his 'desire is to depart and be with Christ, for that is (very) far better'.

This is a very full and remarkable statement about the death of a Christian. He teaches us first about the nature of Christian death: it is 'to depart'. It is possible that this is a camping metaphor. Paul, the old 'tent-maker' (Acts 18: 3), resorts to the language of his trade. In this case, death for the Christian is the end of what was at best a transitory thing, a camp-life, in which he travelled, without permanent resting-place and without sure foundation. This is to be exchanged (2 Cor. 5: 1 ff.) for the 'house not made with hands, eternal in the heavens'. Camp-life is exchanged at death for home-life with Christ. But there is greater wealth of meaning in the other possibility that this 'departing' is a 'weighing of the anchor', a 'setting sail'. Never has this been given better expression than by Bishop Moule in his comment on 2 Timothy 4: 6 where again Paul speaks of his 'departure', '. . . that delightful moment when the friendly flood heaves beneath the freed keel, and the prow is set straight and finally towards the shore of *home,* and the Pilot stands on board, at length "seen face to face." And, lo, as He takes the helm, "immediately the ship is at the land whither they go" (Joh. vi. 21)' (H. C. G. Moule, *A Devotional Commentary*, p. 140).

When a Christian dies all the uncertainties and dangers lie behind: the uncertainties and dangers whether of camp-life or of temporary stay in a foreign port. All the certainties and safeties lie ahead in the presence of Christ. And this, in the second place, is the blessedness of Christian death. Such a one goes to 'be with Christ'. So much about life after death is left, by Scripture, without certain description, but on this central fact there is no hesitation: the Christian dead are 'with Christ'. This is not only the blessedness to which Paul looks forward at the second coming: 'the Lord *himself* will descend . . . so shall we always be *with the Lord*' (1 Thes. 4: 16 f.); 'we await a Saviour, the Lord Jesus Christ' (Phil. 3: 20). As he faced what might well be imminent death this was the centre of his expectation, 'with Christ'.

For our learning he takes the matter just one stage further. He declares, thirdly, the value of death to the Christian: it is (literally) 'by far the best'. Suppose we had been with Paul in Rome just then, and had seen him as he was, a man of immense vigour of mind and body, with gigantic gifts, a man irreplaceable in the church. How keenly we would have felt the loss had the case gone against him and he had been executed! What a tragedy! What an untimely end! And all the other things we hear said when a notable Christian dies unexpectedly. But what is the reality for the person, for Paul? He is not the loser; he is not 'poor Paul'. For him it is better by far than anything else that could have happened or could be imagined: indeed, he is, even as we mourn, the present possessor of unimagined and unimaginable riches (1 Cor. 2: 9). For him, and for us at our death too, it is 'by far the best'.

c. The motive for living (verses 24–26)

With all the heightened sensibilities of an apostle Paul saw and savoured in expectation the glory of being with Christ. He loved the Lord so much more than we do, and therefore all the more yearned for His company and foresaw the marvel of it. Yet, over against all that, he writes three words (only two in Greek) which change the whole picture, 'on your account'. Left to choose for himself and his personal enrichment, death would win hands down. But there is also the Philippian church, and all the others who fill the loving imagination of Paul: what of them? They still need the apostolic hand, and not only is Paul so aware of the dimension of their need that he senses Christ will leave him to meet it (verse 25), but he so loves his fellow Christians and desires their spiritual profit that he is ready for it to be so. What a man the apostle was! The fruitfulness of remaining in this life could hold him as against the superlative joys of living on with Christ!

Thus envisaging that he had yet more time on earth, Paul saw his days as a means not of profit for self but of profit for others—and their spiritual profit at that (verse 25)—and not of glory for self but of glory for Christ when he should be given back to the saints at Philippi (verse 26). No doubt they would surround him with joy and congratulate him on 'winning his case'. But for him the occasion would not be one of self-satisfaction but one of awareness of two dominating motives: 'I live on so that others may grow in Christ, and that Christ may be glorified in me.'

8 THE STEADFAST CHURCH

PAUL'S CONFIDENCE THAT HE WOULD BE ACQUITTED at his trial and set free (verses 25,26) inevitably fell short of an absolute certainty. He apparently so judged the needs of the church of that period that he was as near sure as anyone could be that he would again visit Philippi. Nevertheless, he must prepare the church for either eventuality. Strikingly, one set of instructions sufficed: absent or present, he required that their life should be worthy of the gospel of Christ (verse 27).

This requirement was both exclusive and absolute. The force of the word 'only' is tremendous, as if Paul had said, 'This one thing and this only'. Nothing else was to distract them from this great objective; nothing could excuse them from it; it remained as their primary and all-embracing occupation whether Paul was there or not. The apostolic church is not necessarily a church in which an apostolic person is resident, but it must be a church cast in the apostolic mould. It would be hard to sum up the teaching of verses 12–26 better than to say that Paul's aim and accomplishment was to live 'worthily of the gospel of Christ'. He saw the interests of that gospel as the key to his past (verse 12); he came to decisions in present circumstances by asking what would best tend towards the preaching of Christ (verses 14–18); he made the magnifying of Christ the focus of his future (verse 20). He required that the Philippians should do no less. They must be apostolic.

Paul enforced this exhortation upon the Philippians in a way which would at once have appealed to them. What he said, literally translated, was, 'Behave as citizens worthily of the gospel of Christ.' Philippi was a Roman 'colony' (Acts 16: 22), which was one of the most coveted civic prizes of the Roman Empire. When the status of 'colony' was granted, it meant that those people were reckoned as Roman citizens. Their legal position and privileges were the same as if they lived in Rome itself. They were the homeland in miniature. Paul meant exactly the same when he said that 'our citizenship is in heaven' (3: 20, RV): grace has granted to us the privilege of belonging to a far-off land under whose laws and liberties we, its separated citizens, now live, while we wait for our regathering. In the same sense, the 'life . . . worthy of the gospel' comes to the Philippians as an inescapable obligation. It is the law of the homeland. They cannot claim gospel privileges and evade gospel responsibilities. They cannot claim citizenship of a country whose focal point is 'a Lamb standing, as though it had been slain' (Rev. 5 : 6; 7: 17) and at the same time deny the obligation so to live as to adorn the good news of the Lamb (*cf.* Tit. 2: 10).

In their living of this life, there was one thing which Paul specially longed to hear, that they were steadfast under attack. Paul had found Philippi a place of persecution, and in general the apostolic church was under constant fire. There was great need therefore for this reminder to be unyielding.

I STEADFASTNESS IS GROUNDED IN UNITY (*verses 27,28*)

Paul was immensely practical. He would have had no use for 'a fugitive and cloistered virtue', and the movement of the present verses shows that he never envisaged the worthy life as lived behind protective walls. Three things follow in sequence: live worthily; stand firm; be united. The life worthy of the gospel is like a jewel in a double setting. It is firstly encased in the opposition of the hostile world, against which it must 'stand firm', and this it is enabled to do because of its second setting, fellowship within the unity of the church. In the interests of clarity, let us try to state this another way, for it is most important. Paul, if we may paraphrase him, is saying this: 'My sole objective for you is that you live worthily of the gospel. This means that, whether present or absent, I long for the same news, namely that you are standing firm under attack. But remember that this business of standing firm, while it requires stern resolution on the part of each individual, is a corporate matter, an activity of the fellowship: steadfastness requires your unity of spirit and soul, your co-operative battling for the faith you hold in common.'

Steadfastness is thus grounded in unity. When we examine the unity which Paul is here speaking of, we find that there are four elements in it, and our first task must be to study each separately. To begin with, he speaks of it as *unity of the Spirit*: 'stand firm in one spirit'. It seems best to take this as a reference to the Holy Spirit, for two reasons: negatively, if it does not refer to the Holy Spirit it is very difficult to decide what it does mean, as distinct from the following words 'with one mind'. Of course it could be that Paul is using a phrase like our 'heart and soul', that is, with complete dedication and enthusiasm, but the repetition of the word 'one' is against this: he seems to be enumerating distinct aspects of the unity he desires for them. Positively, the phrase 'stand firm in one Spirit' is paralleled in 4: 1 by the phrase 'stand firm . . . in the Lord', and, as we shall see, the over-all movement and teaching of that later passage is nearly identical with that of the present verses, which makes the parallelism more significant. In 4: 1 their steadfast stand is grounded upon the Lord Jesus. He has them 'in' His possession; they are the recipients of His grace; He is the object of their love and faith, and their common individual and joint possession. In the present passage it is the same essential truth which is expressed by the words 'in one spirit', except that, if anything, there is greater emphasis upon what God has done and is doing for them, to the virtual exclusion of the element of responsive love and faith.

In the balance of New Testament teaching, the Father is the great Architect of salvation, the Son is its Accomplisher, and the Spirit applies to the individual and to the church the benefits which the Father planned and the Son actualized (*cf.* Eph. 1: 4 f., 7, 13 f.; Tit. 1: 2; 2: 11; 3: 5; *etc.*). In the light of this, when Paul pauses first to speak of their unity in the Spirit, he is directing attention to the blessings bestowed upon them by the Spirit who has incorporated them into the church (1 Cor. 12: 13), regenerated them into new life (Jn. 3: 5; Tit. 3: 5), and indwells them in the fullness of divine power (Rom. 8: 11). Their unity is thus, in its essence, something which God has accomplished. It is a given fact about Christians, and as they view a hostile world and wonder about their ability—singly or together—to meet its assaults, Paul counsels: 'Remember what God has done for you; live and grow together in the good things which are your common possession in Christ.'

Paul now proceeds to speak of a *unity of heart and mind*, 'with one mind'. The word here translated 'mind' refers to the sphere of the affections and moral energies. It points to what we feel about things and how we react to them. It raises the question of what things we consider valuable and what constitutes a worthwhile objective in life. It is a single description of that complex of heart, mind, and will which is our experience of ourselves 'on the inside' day by day. If we try to translate this into some word which has bearing on the question of the unity of Christians, we must say that Paul is calling them to *unanimity,* a oneness of emotion, decision, and ambition. We ought to recall that when Paul wrote these words he was not himself experiencing the benefits of a church animated by 'one mind'. Many Christians at Rome were very far from this sort of unanimity with Paul (1: 15–17). In that earlier passage he taught us that the reality of unity is something other than the feeling of oneness. He directed us away from the diversity of emotion to the singleness of message. Yet unity without mutual love, and common interests, and agreed values could be as cold as a marriage of convenience. While it remains an essential unity, and has grasped that one thing without which there is no unity at all, it falls far short of that ideal which Paul holds now before the church at Philippi, as he urges, 'Strive also to feel for each other, to be one in emotion and desire and decision.'

Easily, now, he passes on to *unity in action,* 'striving, side by side'. The church which is experiencing unity must be a church without passengers. Is there unity where there is the tacit or spoken attitude, 'I agree with you but I will not do anything for you', or 'I agree with your aims but I will not go with you to fulfil them'? Acquiescence is not unity; consent is not co-operation; approval is not partnership; a *nem. con.* vote is not enough.

Finally, there is the fourth element in the unity which enables the church to face the world unmoved. It is *unity in the faith,* 'the faith of the gospel'. Clearly this phrase is capable of two meanings.

On the one hand, 'faith' could mean 'believing', and the call to the church is to strive together to bring others to believe in the gospel of Christ, the primary reference being to personal experience. On the other hand, we could understand 'the faith' as the body of belief or of truth in which the gospel is defined, and the call to 'strive for the faith' would be equivalent to 'strive for the truth'. But these two are not exclusive alternatives. They have a common denominator. Whether the church goes out to bring others to faith or is viewed as a body of people holding certain things as true, they are agreed as to what the gospel is. Before a man can preach and invite others to believe, he must know what to preach. There is no agreement unless there is agreement as to what constitutes the gospel. Paul here returns, therefore, to the essential and definitive position adopted in verses 15–18. Indeed, he is doing no more than stress what the New Testament declares throughout, that the unity of the church is a unity in the doctrine and the experience of salvation.

II STEADFASTNESS ISSUES IN CONVICTION (*verses 28–30*)

The united church is considered capable of a resolute stand against the strongest and most fearful opposition. Thus Paul takes his teaching on to the next stage. He sees the Philippian church as 'not frightened in anything by (their) opponents'. Both the main words in this phrase are strong, but the first more so. The church faces 'opponents', 'those who set themselves in opposition', and whose strength is such as to create a panic-stricken stampede, for this is what the word 'frightened' really means. Against such an outcome of the encounter stand the majestic words 'not . . . in anything', a very strong negative. Now when the church faces the world in this way, conviction follows in both the parties concerned.

a. The world sees its true spiritual state

'This (the unmoved church) is a clear omen to them of their destruction.' The problem of producing real spiritual conviction in the unconverted is one that frequently daunts preachers, and it is right that it should, for surely it is a most humbling exercise to estimate the ratio between the number of sermons preached and the number of souls won for Christ. Paul here presents this problem, but against a wider background than the individual sermon, and offers a solution. The problem as he presents it is one touching the quality of the life of the church. Is it a church in which the whole conduct of members is made to turn upon the glory of Christ and the honour of the gospel? Is it a church which is living in the experienced good of its inner unity in Christ? Is it a church facing opposition undaunted? Here is the spring from which the conviction of the unconverted flows.

And what genuine conviction it is! Here is no passing impression, but a dawning of eternal realities—'a proof and omen of destruction'. The word 'destruction' is one of the most awful that Scripture uses, and particularly when one considers that both the noun and the verb are used many times with reference to those who die without Christ and without salvation. To discuss here whether the eternal state of such people is endless conscious separation from God or is, as some hold, to be 'destroyed' in the sense of being 'annihilated', so that they cease to exist in any way at all, would take us too far from our present purpose. Important as such discussion is, we must travel along a by-pass. Either way, 'destruction' is an eternal and irrecoverable state. God, hope, paradise, joy, satisfaction and fulfilment are gone for ever. It is in every way the opposite of the 'salvation' of which this verse also speaks and which Christians will eternally enjoy.

Here indeed is conviction of sin: a man or woman gripped by the awfulness of eternal loss, separated from Christ. It is the product of seeing a church standing for Christ, standing for eternal things, enduring worldly loss and disrepute because of the greater riches which it has found in the Spirit, and in Christian fellowship, and in the faith of the gospel.

b. The Christian sees his true spiritual state

Assurance comes to the Christian from the same experience as brought conviction to the world. He is given a sign, omen, and proof '. . . of your salvation, and that from God' (verse 28). Salvation here has the same comprehensive meaning which we noted in commenting on 1 : 19. It sums up all the blessings that are ours by the plan of God, through the cross of Christ, by the agency of the Holy Spirit. And the Christian to whom Paul speaks in verse 28 has come to the conviction that all these are his, and that some glad day he will be the conscious possessor of an immense spiritual wealth which now, though he really possesses it, he only partly experiences. What is it that brings this assurance?

It comes, first, from evidence of the reality of the work of grace in them. This is stated in the explanation in verse 29; the word 'for' looks back to the word 'clear omen'. You have a clear proof that salvation has come to you from none other than God Himself 'for it has been granted to you that for the sake of Christ you should not only believe in him but also suffer for his sake'. The evidence which Paul offers here is twofold: believing in Christ, and suffering for Christ. To believe is only possible through grace—a truth clearly stated in Ephesians 2: 8, 'for by grace you have been saved through faith; and this is not your own doing, it is the gift of God'. And here in Philippians, too, Paul states that 'it has been granted to . . . believe'. Without over-pressing, we may translate, 'It has been given freely and graciously as a favour of God . . . to believe on him.' But alongside this evidence, which surely we find clear enough, Paul places another evidence which we would hardly have considered in this light: 'God has given you grace to believe . . . also to suffer for his sake.' The suffering which comes to a Christian as a Christian, far from being evidence of divine forgetfulness, as we in our easy rebellion often understand it, is rather 'sign, omen, and proof' of the reality of the work of grace, for 'all who desire to live a godly life in Christ Jesus will be persecuted' (2 Tim. 3: 12).

Christian confidence of salvation comes, secondly, from comparison with apostolic experience, for when the Philippians are 'engaged in the same conflict which you saw and now hear to be mine' (verse 30) they will know that their experience of the hostility of the world and of the ability to stand against it is one of the hall-marks of apostolic Christianity. The life worthy of the gospel of Christ could not be a sheltered experience for them any more than for him. Conflict would be the order of the day, but when out of conflict they purchased victory, standing in one Spirit, with one mind, jointly contending for the faith of the gospel, they would not only see that gospel eating with convicting power into the opposing world, they would also find the Spirit witnessing with their spirits that they were indeed the children of God, and if children, then heirs, heirs of God, joint heirs with Christ, now suffering with Him, but soon to share His glory (Rom. 8: 16 f.).

9 THE WORTHY LIFE

THERE IS MORE BLESSING for the Bible student in the word 'therefore' (RSV 'so') than in any other single word of Scripture! For it makes him stop, and look back to some preceding cause before he moves forward to some following effect. We find the word at the opening of chapter two of Philippians, and it is because of this word and the connection of thought which it makes that we call this study 'The Worthy Life'.

The title is, of course, a deliberate reminiscence of 1: 27, 'Only let your manner of life be worthy of the gospel of Christ.' If we go back to that verse we shall see that Paul does not tell us there what the 'life worthy of the gospel' is. He tells us instead what the outcome of such a life is: his call to the worthy life has a purpose, 'that whether I come and see you or am absent, I may hear . . . that you stand firm'. The worthy life issues in the steadfast life, and Paul's teaching on steadfastness takes him to the end of chapter one. Consequently, when he writes the word 'so' or 'therefore' we see that he is taking up again the theme of worthiness which he had earlier announced.

A paraphrase of his thought may help to display this more clearly: 'I have one single desire (verse 27), and it is that your daily life matches the worth of the gospel. Without such a life you will never face the world and hold your ground, strengthened by what God has done for you, unanimous, jointly at work for the common faith. But such steadfastness has worth-while results: it will convict the world and yourselves also (verse 28), though in different ways! The world it condemns; the church it confirms (verses 29,30). Therefore (verse 1) make my joy full (verse 2) by being of the same mind. . . .'

By this summary we can see that the word 'only' in 1: 27 is repeated in another form by 'complete my joy' in 2: 2, and the 'so' or 'therefore' links the two together. We see also what the central characteristic of the worthy life is: 'Only (1: 27) . . . complete my joy (2: 2) by being of the same mind. . . .' It is the life of unity. Two things help us to see how important this was to Paul, and if we can start by sharing his point of view it will lead us to a more urgent consideration of what he is teaching us. First, he has already dwelt on the topic of unity in 1: 27 as the necessary equipment against a hostile world, but now he returns to it again. It was not enough to say it once; it must be said again, and said in a different way. For if 1: 27 is all we are told about unity then it is simply an aspect of Christian expediency, something useful in achieving a purpose, a tool for a task: unity in order that the world may believe. Paul's repetition of the subject not only underlines its importance but lifts it to a higher level: unity is not just a useful weapon against the world, but rather it belongs to the very essence of Christian life for it is the way in which Christians display outwardly what the gospel is and means to them. Unity is the gospel's hall-mark; it says to all who examine it, 'This life is worthy of the gospel.'

Secondly, Paul says, concerning the life of unity, 'Complete my joy.' What a man the apostle was! Were we in prison, chained, guarded, unjustly accused, vilified by those who ought to be our friends, with no present comfort and no guaranteed future, what would our joy be? Paul's was first spiritual, secondly occupied with the welfare of others, thirdly engrossed in the topic of unity. 'I will need no further happiness,' he says, 'if only I can hear that you are a united church.' It may well be that he sensitively felt the damage and disgrace of the disunity at Rome (1: 15 ff.). It may well be that he dreaded further growth of disquieting features of Philippian life (4: 2). Leaving all such speculations and prudential considerations aside, what we are positively taught is this: the life worthy of the gospel is a life of unity; the life of unity matches the apostolic ideal for the church.

Needless to say, Paul meant a very specific sort of unity. It was not his way to leave abstract notions like unity without definition, and his procedure in the present case is typical of what he does many times over in his letters: first the facts and then the exhortations. Verse 1 gives us the facts, for the word 'if' must not be allowed to import uncertainty into what Paul wrote. He intended, 'If, as is certainly the case . . .' and he proceeded to declare four things which are true about every Christian and which lay a factual foundation on which the life of unity is raised up. The exhortations begin in verse 2 and are at first corporate, and then (verses 3,4) individual.

1 CHRISTIAN ONENESS (*verse 1*)

Before the life of unity can be lived there must be certain things which can be assumed as true about those who are to live in unity. When these things are true they exercise a pressure upon the person about whom they are true, urging him into united living with others. In order to illustrate this meaning, let us take as an example, one of the four items. When he says 'if there is . . . any participation in the Spirit', or, better, RV 'any fellowship of the Spirit', Paul is saying this: 'the work of the Holy Spirit is to create a fellowship (*cf.* 2 Cor. 13: 14), both between the believer and God, and between believers; if such a fellowship has been created in Philippi (and I know it has) then can you resist my appeal to live at one?' The *fact* of a divinely created fellowship carries with it the implication of a church at one with itself.

It is only right to say that commentators differ widely in their understanding of verse 1, and what is offered here is only an individual view of the verse but, with this warning, let us note that the order of the first three items in the verse is the same as that of the 'grace' in 2 Corinthians 13: 14, 'Christ . . . love . . . Spirit. . . .' Indeed, the concluding phrase, 'fellowship of the Spirit' is virtually identical. May it not be, therefore, that Paul is reminding the Philippians here of the great Trinitarian activity of salvation whereby they are 'in Christ', experience the reality of God's love, and have been woven into a fellowship of which the Holy Spirit is both Author and Indweller?

Paul separates this out into three strands and allows each one in turn to exercise its 'pull' on his readers. If they are in Christ, there is a 'comfort' or (better) an 'exhortation' or 'encouragement' which they possess. If they know the love of God, they cannot sidestep its 'consolation' or 'constraint'. If they have been made into a fellowship by the Spirit, can they live in any other way but in fellowship? We can best understand the nouns 'comfort' and 'consolation' if we observe them at work as verbs in 1 Thessalonians 2: 11 f.: 'like a father . . . we *exhorted* and *encouraged* you and charged you to lead a life worthy of God.' In the present passage, however, Paul does not speak of any exhortation or encouragement which he might bring to bear upon the Philippians, but the plain *duty* and *summons* which arises out of what God has done for them. By grace they are (all together and each individually) 'in Christ'. It is their duty and their happy lot to display outwardly this inner unseen unity. Through Christ, the love of God has come to them as an experienced warmth; can they bask in its comfort and not extend it through themselves to their fellow Christians (*cf.* Mt. 18: 32–35; 1 Jn. 4: 11)? This experience of the Son and of the Father has come to them through the gracious work of the Holy Ghost, uniting them with God and with each other. The reality of this fellowship must be shown by a life of practised unity.

What, now, of the fourth item, 'affection and sympathy'? In themselves, these words speak of the root and the fruit. 'Affection' points to the inner source of the emotions, as the old translation 'bowels' shows, being equivalent to our use of the 'heart' as the seat of feelings. 'Sympathy' is the feelings themselves, the emotions going out to their object. Here Paul turns to the human side in the matter of salvation. The man or woman who is the object of the saving activity of Father, Son, and Holy Spirit, is made thereby into a new creature, with a new heart and new objectives. 'If this is true of you Philippians,' Paul says, 'then you have a renewed, new-created heart out of which new emotions will flow, and in particular tender, sympathetic and compassionate feelings.' Here again is a motive and spring of unity.

Unity is supremely important, but it is a by-product. It arises out of other matters. Two great presuppositions must be made, and made with truth and reality, before the call to unity can go forth. There must be agreement in the doctrine and experience of salvation before there can be the manifested unity of living in fellowship. Paul taught this in 1: 15 ff. and he has now returned to it again, and it shines out through the New Testament. The doctrine of salvation is stated here in its classical Trinitarian form (*cf.* Eph. 1: 4,7,13 f.; 1 Pet. 1: 2; 2 Thes. 2: 13 f.; Tit. 3: 4 ff.; *etc.*). If people do not agree in their acceptance and understanding of the saving work of Father, Son, and Holy Ghost they cannot be at one. It is essential to use the words 'acceptance *and understanding*', for the emphasis on the 'mind' in verse 2 will not allow us to say that unity can go forward merely because people, in some undefined way, look to the Trinity as the source and means of salvation. A doctrinal agreement is required, a real *knowledge* of the work of God, and, of course, that means something that is held by head and heart alike, something grasped intellectually and lived out practically. Hence Paul did not let the matter rest until he had brought it down to the intimately personal and individual level of 'affection and sympathy'. Here is the greatness of salvation in its application and experience. Unity cannot proceed on head-knowledge alone; there must also be the personal acceptance of it as the means of 'my salvation' (*cf.* Eph. 1: 13) and, therefore, as the ground of unity with those who have a 'like precious faith' (*cf.* 2 Pet. 1: 1, RV).

II CHRISTIAN UNISON (*verse 2*)

If a choir is to sing in unison, it takes no great effort to achieve it, but in a congregation, with its varied talents, and sometimes entire absence of musical talent, a more conscious dedication to the task is required. As we have followed Paul's teaching so far in this chapter of Philippians, we have seen that before he called the church to unity of life he dwelt upon the great facts which make Christians at one. But, at the same time, while he saw unity as a by-product of these facts, he certainly did not see it coming as automatically as, say, tar arises in the production of coal-gas or 'golden syrup' in the refining of sugar. If unison (and this word possibly describes the contents of verse 2 better than does 'unity') is to be achieved, there is need of an exhortation. It will not 'come naturally', however natural it is in relation to the gospel. It will only come by effort, by obedience to the apostolic call, by deliberately living out and cultivating that sort of life which is worthy of the good news that the Holy Trinity is God the Redeemer.

In verse 2 we cannot help being struck by the 'inwardness' of

Paul's requirements. When he wrote about unity in 1: 27 he at least included 'striving side by side', but now all is occupied with the mind (twice), with love, and with 'accord', a word which conceals the same idea as 'with one mind' in 1: 27. In other words Christian unison involves the person as a person, right in the inmost recesses of his being. We may put it this way: true Christian unison is not just my getting on with him and he with me; it is the identity of our two persons. Once more, unity is a by-product: it grows out of inner oneness. An example chosen from what Paul says here will help towards clarity. He speaks of 'the same love'. What does this mean in respect of unity? It means that there can never be real Christian unity and fellowship where there is inner antipathy, and Christians should make this inner reality of unison their aim.

In order to avoid involving the apostle in a contradiction while we attempt to understand his teaching, we must pause here to recall that in 1: 15–17 we saw that he did not try to solve the problems of unity by means of the doctrine of sanctification. But are we not saying here that without complete sanctification, for example, love identical with God's love, we cannot be one? This is true. The fellowship and unity of heaven will utterly transcend even the best we have known on earth, for it will be the fellowship of the completely sanctified. This is our *aim* on earth but not our *solution*. I cannot say 'if only he were more holy I could get on with him', for he could *with equal truth* say it of me! Therefore the more objective realities of the doctrine and personal experience of salvation are the solution to problems of unity, being stated here just as clearly as in 1: 15 ff., and on this basis we are to strive after that deeper unity of persons.

Paul's emphasis is upon the unison of *minds*. He says we are to be 'of the same mind . . . of one mind' or, more literally, 'think the same thing . . . thinking the one thing'. Agreement in the truth is a priority task. But within this there is unity in *love*: 'having the same love'. The emphasis here is on love as one of the elements in our inner make-up. He does not say that we are to 'love the same things' but to 'possess the same love', and what can this be but a love identical with that which God has bestowed upon us, so that we are moved and react as He would, and, by thus being conformed to a common standard, united with each other? It is also unity of *accord*. The word, literally translated, is 'like-souled', and resembles the 'with one mind' of 1: 27. The 'soul' has been defined as 'the sphere of the affections and moral energies', and if this is so we may say that Paul is here calling for a unity of will in God's people, for 'love' expresses unity of emotion or affection and the remaining word could well take up the other idea. In this way, he calls Christians to an inner unison of mind, emotion, and will. The practical aspect of this 'tall order' occupies him from verse 5 onwards, but before we consider that there is one remaining aspect of the worthy life which we must observe.

III CHRISTIAN HARMONY (*verses 3,4*)

A new feature appears in verses 3 and 4, which, although not absent from verse 2, as we shall see, was not explicitly mentioned. It is the word 'each', which appears in both verses in RV. We could not draw out the meaning of verse 2 without speaking of 'me' and 'him', and so on. Nevertheless the verbs remained plural and the individual was still an implication. Now the individual is in the centre of the picture. The responsibility for the worthy life of unity is individual, personal, mine.

Actually verse 3 has no verb and could well be taken in with the plural of verse 2, as in the RV, 'doing nothing. . . .' It is better, however, to take it as part of the statement of individual responsibility, and in this case we find in turn a wrong attitude towards oneself in the realm of aims ('selfishness', 'faction' or 'self-seeking'), and in the realm of assessment ('conceit' or 'vainglory'), followed by a correct attitude towards oneself in the realm of assessment ('humility') and in the realm of aims (each looking 'to the interests of others', verse 4).

Looking back, we can picture Paul's teaching from 1: 27 to 2: 4 as an upturned triangle. The long line at the top is the place where the church faces the world, finds it hostile but yet stands fast. But this steadfastness depends on the strength of the 'legs' which support it, and they are not 'splayed out' for strength, but triangle-wise come to a point—the point of individual responsibility. Paul does not leave the question of the worthy life which produces the steadfast stand until he brings it to rest on the worthy life as it is found in the individual, a man not of self-seeking conceitedness, but with a correctly humble estimate of himself, seeking the welfare of others and putting them first. Steadfastness depends on unity, and unity depends on me.

10 THE CHRISTIAN'S MODEL

THIS PASSAGE IS VIRTUALLY UNIQUE in the Bible. Four times over, in the Gospels, we find the history of the cross of Christ; time and again the Epistles turn to their favourite theme, the meaning of the cross, the wonder of its effect, the remission of our sins. But rarely does Scripture open to us the thoughts and motives of the Son of God as He contemplated the cross, and this is the speciality of these verses. We see the work of redemption as He saw it. We see the cross through the eyes of the Crucified. We enter into the 'mind' of Christ. But we do well to remember that we are privileged to enter the mind of Christ not for the satisfaction of our curiosity but for the reformation of our lives. Paul has called the church to worthy living, issuing in steadfastness under fire, and depending on individuals with correct assessments of themselves and correct aims in living. 'What am I calling you to?' he cries. 'To this: let this mind be in you which was also in Christ.' The vital element in the church on earth is the individual fashioned after the likeness of his Lord in an identity of *mind,* for it is out of the inner man that the rest of the life flows.

The revelation of the 'mind of Christ' is given here in the story of a *great change*. It begins with One who was 'in the form of God' (verse 6). We associate the word 'form' with outward shape, and it does not lose that meaning in the Bible. But we also sometimes attach another meaning to it: 'Are you in good form today?' Here the same word has a different meaning. It points inward; it asks about hidden matters. Now both these meanings seem to converge when it is said that Christ Jesus was 'in the form of God'. It means that He possessed inwardly and displayed outwardly the very nature of God Himself. The word translated 'form' is not in fact often used in the New Testament, but its meaning is well exemplified when it appears as a verb in Galatians 4: 19 where Paul describes himself as in travail for the Galatians 'until Christ be formed in you', that is, until inwardly and outwardly, in thought as well as in life, you are (so to speak) 'conformed' to Him (*cf.* Phil. 3: 10,21). Likewise, the Lord Jesus Christ was 'in the form of God', inwardly possessing the divine nature, outwardly displaying the divine glory.

The same truth is elsewhere taught concerning the Lord Jesus, and it will help to fix it in our minds, and to sharpen our appreciation of the great change to which He committed Himself if we dwell on some verses. We read in Colossians 1: 15 that He 'is the image of the invisible God'. He is the one in whom the essential, spiritual nature of God Himself is given outward display. Hebrews 1: 3 makes it clearer. He is 'the effulgence of his glory' (RV), the one in whom the inner radiance of God, who is Light (1 Jn. 1: 5), shines out; but also He is 'the very stamp (RV mg. 'the impress') of his nature', as though the nature of God were a seal impressed upon wax. Again, 2 Corinthians 4: 4 speaks of 'Christ . . . the likeness of God' and verse 6 of the experience of seeing 'the glory of God in the face of Christ'. And there are many more such references, but the underlying truth becomes clear as we contemplate even these few: the Lord Jesus—and in Philippians 2: 6 we must remember that Paul is speaking of the Lord before the incarnation—possessed inwardly and displayed outwardly the very nature of God.

What a change therefore is represented by verse 8, where we read that He 'became obedient unto death'! We simply cannot achieve any logical understanding of this:

'Tis mystery all! The immortal dies.

But, mysterious though it may be, it is the testimony of the Bible. We remember the accusation made by Peter: 'You . . . asked for a murderer to be granted to you, and *killed the Author of life*.' There is the mystery in a nutshell, 'killed . . . life'. Paul himself dwells on the same truth in 1 Corinthians 2: 8, '. . . crucified the

Lord of glory'. A glance back over the references recently given will show that the word 'glory' means much more than simply 'splendour'. It has the idea of the outshining nature of God. This was the Lord whom they crucified! How could it ever happen? We cannot tell how, but we know that it did happen.

Having thus tried to see the great change which took place, we may observe next that it came about by voluntary decision. Here is the beginning of that perception of the 'mind of Christ' which Paul was inspired by the Holy Spirit to emphasize. It was the 'mind of Christ' by an act of deliberate choice to bring His glory down into the dust of death. According to verse 7, He 'emptied himself'; verse 8 records that 'he humbled himself'. Those commentators who concern themselves directly with the Greek text urge a special significance in the order of words in verse 7, where it reads, literally, 'himself he emptied', the object coming before the subject, and where 'the emphatic position of "himself" points to the humiliation of our Lord as voluntary, self-imposed' (Lightfoot).

This 'mind' of voluntary self-humbling stands more sharply revealed if we consider the phrase which sets the situation and the decision of Christ before us. He 'did not count equality with God a thing to be grasped' (verse 6). The meaning of this phrase has vexed every commentator on Philippians, and it is not part of our intention here to try to solve it! The present approach is governed by considering that if there are two or more possible meanings, then it is reasonable to suppose that Paul knew this to be so, but was content that each alike expressed an acceptable truth. In general, in the present case, the commentators find three lines of approach. The problem centres upon the meaning of the Greek word which the RSV translates 'a thing to be grasped', RV 'a prize' and the AV 'robbery'.

a. It can mean 'a possession to be held on to at all costs'. In this case, the possession is 'equality with God'. Once the Jews 'sought . . . to kill him, because he . . . called God his Father, making himself equal with God'. The phrase is almost identical with that which Paul uses in Philippians. However, in John 5: 18 it is the truth of personal equality which is expressed, the word 'equal' being masculine in gender. In Philippians 2: 6 it is neuter plural, 'to be equal things with God'. The reference in this case is to the Son's co-possession with the Father of the eternal divine glory, that glory which, in His incarnate state, He longed to have restored, 'Glorify thou me in thy own presence with the glory which I had with thee before the world was' (Jn. 17: 5). As far as we are concerned, these are merely words. The reality behind them is beyond our comprehension. We do not possess the categories whereby we might bring such eternal glories within the range of our finite powers. To us they are words, but to Him a superb and loved reality which He freely surrendered in the interests of a greater purpose. This is the 'mind of Christ': to take the best and the greatest which the self knows and desires, and to abandon it in a voluntary act of self-denial.

b. Others urge that the word means 'a position which could be exploited'. We may feebly illustrate this by comparing the shopkeeper who trades on a busy corner of a main street with the shopkeeper making his bare living in a scarcely used side-turning. The former possesses a platform for allowable self-advancement. He holds a position which he can exploit. Before considering this explanation any further, it will be well to state the third possibility, for the two can then be bracketed together.

c. 'A thing to be grasped for self, as a robber grasps his loot.' The connecting link between these two explanations is the suggestion that the Son of God, prior to His incarnation, could have reached out after further glories beyond those which He already possessed. His being 'in the form of God' gave Him a unique opportunity for self-aggrandizement. In considering the possibility of this explanation, we clearly need to walk with great care and reverence. We are speaking once again of a mystery, the relations between the Persons of the eternal Trinity. However, it is clear that there is a 'primacy' of the Father in the Trinity. We read in Ephesians 1: 3 of 'the *God* and Father of our Lord Jesus Christ'. Or, again, in John 20: 17, the risen Lord speaks of '*my God* and your God'. Likewise, in the often quoted Mark 13: 32, He says that 'of that day or that hour no one knows, not even the angels in heaven, nor the Son, but only the Father'. We must notice that He does not say 'neither do I know it', as though this lack of knowledge was a feature of His condition when on earth; He says that this knowledge is kept from 'the Son'—not the One made a little lower than the angels (Heb. 2: 9) but the

Son who is above them. Thus the Lord Jesus hinted to us something of the relation between the Persons of the Godhead. Was it then possible for the Son to contemplate using His favoured and unique position in an act of personal gain and exploitation?

The most fruitful and helpful approach to this question is along the line of the comparison between the first and the second Adam. Up to a point the likeness is most remarkable. Three great descriptive words which have already appeared in our study of the Lord Jesus Christ are also used of Adam: he was the son of God (Lk. 3: 38), and the image and glory of God (Gn. 1: 26; 1 Cor. 11: 7). In addition, he had a unique position in the paradise of God: to him was given dominion (Gn. 1: 28), and the law of God (Gn. 2: 16 f.). The great question is this: how will he use his uniqueness? As a position to be exploited for personal gain? Furthermore, how will he view those additional glories which the wisdom of God has hitherto forbidden to him—the eating of the tree of the knowledge of good and evil? Will he see this as the object of a personal act of robbery, of snatching and holding for self? These are the compelling questions of Genesis 3.

The answers are tragic. The first Adam was manoeuvred by the serpent into the position of exploiting for his own gain his favoured position of access to the forbidden tree, and of grasping for self-aggrandizement that which the divine sovereignty had withheld. But the essential tragedy was this, that when he thus, in a spirit of self-seeking, grasped after fuller life, he actually laid hold upon death: 'In the day that you eat of it you shall die.' And here, precisely, is the revelation of the mind of Christ, that He deliberately did the exact opposite! Whether in fact such a choice was ever presented to Him in His heavenly glory, we are not told. But we are told how He acted in respect of that glory and in respect of the possibility of self-enrichment it offered, and in respect of further glory beyond what He possessed. He chose the way of self-emptying, self-humbling, not grasping after 'equal things' with God, but deliberately setting Himself on the path of self-denial. Where the first Adam reached out after life but actually laid hold on death, the second Adam turned His back on life and voluntarily laid hold on death. And this, says Paul, is the 'mind of Christ'.

There does not seem to be any way of deciding which of these two interpretations is the more correct. But if we try to grasp both at once we have a wonderfully vigorous and emphatic notion of that way of looking at things and of going about things which Paul says was the mark of Christ and should therefore be the mark of all who are in Christ and are concerned to be like Him. Self-advantage is not a thing to be held at all costs; profit for self is not the guiding consideration for future conduct; the desire to grasp and hold for self is not the overriding objective in moments of choice. Rather the contrary. The mind of Christ is to reject all this, deliberately and decisively, and patiently to take the course which is dictated by the rejection of self, the way of dying to all that self stands for.

The spring from which this passage originates is Paul's call for a 'life . . . worthy of the gospel' (1: 27). The worthy life produces steadfastness; the worthy life is the life of unity; the worthy life is the task of the individual. To these truths which have emerged from our study up to 2: 4 there is now added the supreme truth: the worthy life is the life of Christ, arising out of a mind patterned upon His; the task of the individual in the church is to look on his fellow believers through the eyes of Christ and to act towards them on the same principles on which Christ Jesus has acted towards him.

11 THREE MINDS

WE HAVE LOOKED IN A PRELIMINARY WAY at our Lord Jesus Christ's attitude towards Himself and towards the cross, and we have seen how Paul viewed this as setting a pattern for the individual Christian within the fellowship of the church. Our concern in the present study is not to add essentially to this truth, but to attempt to display it on a larger scale as it is worked out in the complete passage.

I THE MIND OF CHRIST (*verses 6–8*)

We have already seen that the mind of Christ is displayed here through a marvellous and voluntarily accepted change from life to death.

Closer examination of the verses shows that this change is brought about in two stages. This can be seen by considering the end of verse 7 and the beginning of verse 8, two phrases of a parallel nature. In verse 7, we read that He was 'born in the likeness of men', that is to say, Paul has at this point traced the story of the Lord Jesus to the point of His 'becoming flesh' (Jn. 1: 14). Then in verse 8, he resumes from the same point, saying, 'And being found in human form. . . .' Thus, the earthly life of our Lord is both a stopping-place and a starting-place in the story of the change which He willingly experienced. From one point of view what could be greater than that God became man? And yet there is something greater, something far and away more marvellous and unpredictable. We will follow Paul as he conducts us through this mighty narrative.

a. The Eternal becomes incarnate (verses 6,7)
The One who was 'in the form of God' took the 'form of a servant'. We start with something that was His *by right*. The word which verse 6 translates as 'was' is found, for example, in Acts 16: 20, 'these men are Jews'. It occurs again in 1 Corinthians 11: 7, 'since he *is* the image and glory of God'. It is not the Greek verb 'to be', stating a fact of existence, but another verb which means 'to be *by nature*' as, for example, that a man is a Jew, or is in the image of God. In this sense, as a very fact of His personal Being, Christ was 'in the form of God'. He possessed inwardly and displayed outwardly the divine attributes.

But, being so, He emptied Himself! We cannot avoid the question which is as logical as it is enticing: emptied Himself of what? The passage provides an answer to this question only if the first of the explanations of the word 'prize' or 'robbery' is true. For it is clear, as the Lord Jesus Himself inferred in John 17: 5, that He left behind the glory which He shared with the Father before the world was. It was part of His self-denying 'mind' to strip off from Himself the 'equal things', the shared riches of the heavenly places. But that He ceased to be God, or that He stripped Himself of any divine *attributes* (as distinct from outward manifestations of divine glory) is not suggested by this passage, and is strongly denied by every page of the gospel record.

In point of fact, however, to ask of what He emptied Himself is to be guided by logic rather than by the course which these verses themselves take. For here the 'emptying' is described as 'taking' the form of a servant, and 'being born' or 'becoming' in the likeness of man. We should see the idea of 'emptying', therefore, not in its logical implication of discarding something, but rather in the light of Isaiah 53: 12, 'He *poured out* his soul to death', with the double idea of total personal committal, and complete personal subjection. Even so, the Lord Jesus Christ, in the totality of His divine nature, completely committed and submitted Himself to a wholly other mode of being: the 'form of a servant', the inner and outer reality of being a slave. The Son became the bondservant.

Here, again, is the mind of Christ: the eternal glories, His by nature and by right, are not the platform for self-display, or self-advantage, but for self-denial. Self, to Him, was something to 'pour out'.

b. The Incarnate becomes a curse (verse 8)
But wonderful as the incarnation is, a greater thing is to follow. Verse 7 teaches that the 'emptying' was achieved by taking on a new experience. Just as, in Isaiah 53, the Servant of the Lord poured himself out by accepting death into his experience, so Jesus, the Servant, 'came-to-be in the likeness of men'. He adopted a new mode of existence which had not been His before. Verse 8 continues from this point. He who experienced what it was to be 'in the likeness of men' was 'found in human form'. Those meeting Him felt the presence of a man: He looked like one, and, for the most part, acted like one, so that they could say, 'Is not this the carpenter?' (Mk. 6: 3). But how much of the truth they thus missed! Well might Isaiah say, 'To whom has the arm of the Lord been revealed?'—or, as we might paraphrase, 'Who would have believed that this was God Himself come down to save?' Certainly, He was 'likeness' and 'form' of man; but He was also God. Let us notice how Paul says in verses 5,6 that it was 'Christ *Jesus*' who pre-existed in eternity as possessor of the very nature of God. But 'Jesus' is the name of 'the carpenter'! That is to say, there is personal identity and continuity between the pre-existing and the incarnate Son of God.

Lo, within a manger lies
He who built the starry skies.

We are now in a position to see that the Eternal in becoming incarnate still retains what we may call a platform for self-display, self-advantage, self-glorification. He *seems* the same as other men, but how vastly different in fact He is! May He not use this unique position, that of God-man, to make some gain for self? This was certainly the proposition put to Him by Satan in the wilderness. Could He not use His power for self-advantage by turning stones into bread? Could He not exploit His protected status as Son of God by leaping unhurt from the Temple tower? Could He not win all the glory and allegiance of the world for Himself by a simple act of bowing to Satan? Truly, the Second Adam met the same enemy as the first! Indeed, it may be that in a different way the same sort of course opened before Him on the Mount of Transfiguration: that, having received the plaudits of the greatest of the men who preceded Him, and the accolade from God Himself, He could, on His own merits, step back into the personal glory of heaven.

What, in fact, He did was very different from all this. He took upon Him the one thing which, without His consent, had no power against Him—death (Jn. 10: 18). His uniqueness was His immortality, that which properly and exclusively belongs to God (1 Tim. 6: 16). It was the very acme of His distinctness and superiority over all other men. Here was the means of self-glorification and self-display had He desired such. But He went, instead, the way of death, 'carrying His obedience even as far as death itself'. And even that was not the end, for Paul adds, 'even death on a cross'. His death involved Him in the negation not only of that which made Him distinct among men, but also of that which was His supreme distinctiveness, 'the form of God'. For we read that 'cursed be every one who hangs on a tree'. He who from all eternity possessed and displayed the divine attributes ended His incredible career of self-abasement under the curse of God.

Paul does not say here what he says often elsewhere, but we cannot forbear to add the words, 'And He did it for me!' All this unbelievable energy of self-abasement, from the highest glory of the eternally shared splendour of the Father's love down to the dust of death and the awfulness of the curse of a sin-hating God. And all for love of a sinner like me!

But what Paul does say and emphasize ought equally to capture our attention and reverent acceptance. This is the 'mind of Christ'. Everything touching self-advantage or conducing to self-display must go. There is no limit to self-humbling as long as anything remains which may be poured out.

II THE MIND OF GOD (*verses 9–11*)

We have now seen something of the 'mind of Christ', His attitude towards things, the motives and purposes which He accepts as governing Himself. As we follow the verses, Paul now has a further 'mind' to reveal to us: the reaction of God to all this. God observed the mind of His Son; He saw the extent to which His

Son offered Him obedience—even to death, so obedient was He! What does God think?

The word 'therefore' (verse 9) ought to be pondered. It tells us two things: first, that the action of God now to be related (verses 9–11) was a *reaction*. It was not simply something which He did, but a response He made. Secondly, we learn that this reaction was, in His judgment, the exact recompense which the work of His Son merited. Consequently, when we study this act of God we are permitted to see into the mind of God. The outward act is the product of His all-wise assessment, executed by means of His almighty power. In other words, it is an exact reward.

There are three aspects of this responsive act of God. We note, in the first place, that God made Jesus the Possessor of the supreme Name (verse 9). In the Bible, a name usually has a double significance. On the one hand, it is a public designation, that is, a name in the same sense that each of us is given a name. It is something by which others know us. But the Bible, on the other hand, very frequently insists that a man's name has a much more personal significance also: that it describes the character or nature of the person who bears the name (*e.g.* 1 Sa. 25: 25; Mt. 1: 21). God's first response, then, was to bestow on His Son a public designation which exactly matched His personal nature and character. What is this Name? Some say that it is the name Jesus, itself, and that the responsive act of God was to make this name—and therefore its Possessor—the supreme One over all. But the phrase 'gave unto him the name' would rather suggest some new act of God, and not merely the authentication of some already existing situation.

A better interpretation is that the Name given is 'Lord', which, in the Old Testament, would be Jehovah or (better) Yahweh, the personal name of God Himself. Three features of the present passage support this interpretation. First, no name other than Yahweh has a right to be called 'the name above every name'. Secondly, the movement of verses 9–11 does not stop at the phrase 'gave him the name . . .', but flows straight on to the universal confession that 'Jesus Christ is Lord', which suggests that the significant thing is the ascription of 'Lord' *in addition* to the names already known. Thirdly, verse 10 is a pretty direct quotation of Isaiah 45: 23, where Yahweh, having declared Himself to be the only God and the only Saviour, vows that He will yet be the Object of universal worship and adoration. It is this divine honour that is now bestowed upon the Lord Jesus Christ.

But what does this mean? Was He not always God? Certainly! Nevertheless, in the Old Testament He was God incognito! We who possess the New Testament are inclined to say that such figures in the Old Testament as 'the angel of the Lord'—some would even say such a mysterious figure as Melchizedek (Gn. 14)—were in fact early revelations of the Second Person of the Trinity, and that at every time it was He who interposed between God and men. But let us ask this question. With only the Old Testament in our hands would we ever know Him as the Second Person, or would we know that the Angel of the Lord was to be the Messiah, or that His name would be Jesus? It is in this sense that we say that in the Old Testament He was God incognito. But now He is God, publicly proclaimed, publicly possessing the only Name which could completely say who and what He is: Jesus is Lord. Jesus is Jehovah. Jesus is Yahweh.

The second responsive act of God was to appoint Jesus to be the Object of universal worship (verses 10,11a). The significance of this can be summed up in the dramatic phrase, 'The triumph of the Crucified'. At this very moment, Jesus, the Possessor of the supreme Nature, is of necessity the Occupant of the throne over all things. Yet, here again, there is an incognito. Many do not recognize this fact; many have never heard of it; many who know it behave as if it were not true; and many reject it altogether. But the crowning day is coming! It will be the day when the incognito will be dropped. It will be the *parousia,* the day of the Lord's visible presence. On that day there will be no dispute as to who is King! John was allowed a preview: 'And I heard every creature in heaven and on earth and under the earth and in the sea, and all therein, saying, "To him who sits upon the throne and to the Lamb be the blessing and honour and glory and might for ever and ever!" And the four living creatures said, "Amen!" and the elders fell down and worshipped' (Rev. 5: 13 f.). And do we not wish ourselves among them? Praise God that it shall be so with joy for all the redeemed!

God's response to the Son's career of self-abasement to death had a third aspect. He designated Jesus as the sole glory of the Father. We may well recall here one of the possible interpretations of 'thing to be grasped' in verse 6. We saw the possibility that the Son had turned His back on any attempt to snatch the supreme glory for Himself. But now it is His, by the responsive will of God. All the glory of the Father is centred in Him, so that in Him and by Him alone is the Father glorified. If we may speak reverently, God the Father has staked His whole reputation upon this Son of His, who obediently left His Father's throne, emptied Himself, and 'bled for Adam's helpless race'. This is the mind of God. He has said, as it were, Give Me one who will go all the way in self-humbling, and in that man I will be glorified.

III THE MIND OF THE CHRISTIAN (*verse 5*)

We have asked the objective question, What did God think of the career of His Son? But the passage will not allow us to evade the personal question, What do you think of it? Indeed, this was Paul's whole purpose in displaying the mind of Christ. If he has treated us to a superb piece of theological writing, we might almost say that he was betrayed into it by his insistence that every Christian should model himself upon Jesus. It is his apostolic command to us which initiates the verses we have been studying, 'Have this mind among yourselves, which you have in Christ Jesus' (verse 5). Paraphrasing, in order to bring out the double-edged meaning, 'You are in Christ; you must be like Christ.'

Here then is the Christian's Model. He turned His back, voluntarily, deliberately, and decisively, upon all that belonged to personal glory, and all that conduced to personal gain. He recognized no limit to the extent to which His obedience to God in self-humbling must go. Whatever He found in Himself to be expendable, He spent. While anything was left which could be poured forth, He poured it forth. Nothing was too small to give, or too great. This is the mind and the life which is commended to us by the example of Christ, and approved by signal acts of God. And 'in Christ' grace is pledged sufficient for the outworking of it.

12 SECRETS ARE FOR SHARING

THE PRECISE CONNECTION OF THESE VERSES with what has gone before will be our concern in the next chapter. For the present it will contribute to a greater fullness of study if we pause to examine certain observations which Paul makes incidentally to his main purpose, and which we may sum up as his four-sided description of what a Christian is like.

I SALVATION

The first of the four elements in the apostolic description of a Christian is that *he possesses salvation.* The present tense, 'possesses', ought to be stressed. Paul says to the Philippian Christians, 'Work out your own salvation', and both the predicate and the object of that sentence imply the present possession of the thing named. He says, not work for, or work towards, but 'work out'. If a person comes to us with a problem, with which, for any reason, we are unable to help them, we might reply, 'I am sorry. I cannot help. You must work it out for yourself.' It is in this sense exactly that 'work out' is an appropriate translation of the verb in verse 12. A person can only 'work out' a problem which he already possesses; a person can only 'work out' a salvation which is already his. For this reason Paul says, '*your own*' salvation, meaning to say, not 'the salvation which will yet be yours provided you work for it', but 'the salvation which is already yours'.

Comparison with another scripture will help us to hold this great truth of Christian certainty, and to strip off from it any objectionable accompaniments of self-conceit or cockiness. The testimony to assured, personal, and present salvation ought to be woven throughout with the threads of profound humility. The verse in question is Ephesians 2: 8. It says, we 'have been saved', and the tense implies a present state of affairs persisting from the past. This salvation rests, on the one side, on the words 'by grace', and, on the other side, on the words 'through faith; and this is not your own doing, it is the gift of God'. The Christian is one who possesses salvation, and whose heart goes out in humble, adoring worship to the God who has accomplished the whole work, in its objective and its subjective aspects alike (*cf.* Phil. 1: 6,29).

II INDWELLING

The second element in the description of a Christian is that *he is indwelt by God* (verse 13). Paul dwells on this truth, telling us five distinct things about it. He starts with an assertion: the *fact* of the divine indwelling. 'God . . . in you.' This was something of an emphasis with him in his letters to Ephesus, Colosse and Philippi. To the Colossians (1: 27) he asserts that 'God chose to make known how great among the Gentiles are the riches of the glory of this mystery, which is Christ in you, the hope of glory'. 'Christ in you'—the fact of divine indwelling. Ephesians 3: 16–19 is the greatest expression of this theme, in the course of his prayer that they may know the fullness of that divine indwelling which is proper to them as Christians: 'that . . . he may grant you to be strengthened with might through his Spirit in the inner man, and that Christ may dwell in your hearts through faith; that you . . . may be filled with all the fullness of God.' 'His Spirit . . . Christ . . . the fullness of God'—here is the fact of divine indwelling. And the teaching stems from the words of the Lord Himself. He promised 'another Counsellor . . . the Spirit . . . (who) will be in you' (Jn. 14: 16,17). But in His coming (verse 18) the Lord Himself would come to them. And, in addition, Father and Son will come to the lovingly obedient one (verse 23) and make Their home with him. Here again, then, is the fact of the divine indwelling.

We next learn the *nature* of the divine indwelling. The indwelling God is 'working': 'for God is at work in you'. In the wonderful balance of Bible teaching, this verse has a great truth to set before us. Doubtless we have all heard sermons at some time or another warning of the possibility of neutralizing (we say it reverently) the presence of God in the life. Christ was in the boat, but while *Peter* took the helm, He slept. This is a necessary truth. Paul himself warns similarly that the Spirit may be grieved (Eph. 4: 30), or 'quenched' (1 Thes. 5: 19). We must not forget these things. We must ever be sensitive to the moral and spiritual conditions on which we *enjoy* the indwelling of God. But, over against all that, Paul here encourages us with a great truth. God will never let His people go; He is ever at work; He never sleeps; He is tirelessly alert; God is (literally translated) 'the working One'. When we forget, He does not forget; when we backslide, He works for our recovery and return. It is God who is 'at work' (*cf.* 1: 6).

And His work is *not in vain*. It is the greatest encouragement to ponder the verses where this verb, 'at work', and its related noun are used, verses such as Ephesians 1: 11,20; 3: 7,20; Philippians 3: 21; Colossians 1: 29; *etc.* There is no uncertainty about this power. 'The verb carries the idea of effectual working' and 'the kindred noun (always in the New Testament of superhuman energy) is "power in exercise"' (Vincent). We may give this opinion of the meaning of the word a brief trial by glancing at Galatians 2: 8, 'He who worked through Peter for the mission to the circumcised worked through me also for the Gentiles.' The Epistle to the Galatians is itself the commentary on this verse. If we would know what this 'working' of God was, then it was that effectual implementation of the will of God by which Paul was chosen before birth (Gal. 1: 15), and called—a word which in the Epistles carries the idea of 'effectually called', the call guaranteeing the response—and ushered, solely by divine authority and activity, into apostleship (Gal. 1: 1). God's working is effectual working. The outcome is guaranteed in the deed. He cannot be defeated. And this God 'is at work in you'. If the truth of present possession of salvation speaks for our assurance, the truth of the indwelling of a sovereign God must be the source of unspeakable comfort to our souls.

The *object* at which this effectual working aims is 'to will and to work'. There are two aspects in every deliberate action: the hidden aspect is the process of decision and choice. Out of all possible actions in a given situation, one must be selected and determined upon. The mind must be set in a particular direction. The other side of action is to carry into effect what has been secretly chosen and decided. In other words, there is purposing, and there is working. Every day, one or other of these is the occasion of our downfall. Either we are unable even to choose what we know to be pleasing to God, or else, having chosen it, we are unable to do it (*cf.* Rom. 7: 18 ff.). Sin has corrupted the power of the will and the power of accomplishment. But God is ceaselessly and effectually at work in the redeemed to recreate the will, in order that it may conform to His will, and to impart a capacity for effectual working—for the same word is used: the effectual Worker Himself would make us like Himself. In this respect, this verse completes a great trio of verses in Philippians which show as clearly as any in the New Testament that the whole work of salvation is God's. According to 1: 29, the faith which we exercised in Christ at the start was God's gracious gift. According to 1: 6 the ultimate goal of completeness in Christ is guaranteed and will be achieved by God's faithful power. And according to the present verse the interim, between the beginning in grace and the consummation in grace, is catered for by the divine Indweller energizing, ceaselessly at work, to effect a perfect will and a perfect work.

Before leaving this question of the divine indwelling, Paul declares what its *motive* is. The cause of this total work of grace, accomplished by the effectual power of the indwelling God, is 'his good pleasure'. The Bible knows no other answer to the deepest of all questions. Why does God bother with sinners? Why did God choose me, and send His Son to die for me?

Jesu, what didst Thou find in me
That Thou hast dealt so lovingly?

Moses, of old, gave the answer, and it has never been either replaced or enlarged upon, 'It was not because you were more in number than any other people that the Lord set his love upon you and chose you . . . but . . . because the Lord loves you' (Dt. 7: 7,8). It is no answer to say that the Lord loves you because He loves you! And yet it is the greatest and best answer, because it means that though the reasons are hidden from us they are reasons which *seem good to God*. They are therefore eternally valid reasons, and 'neither death, nor life, nor angels, nor principalities, nor things present, nor things to come, nor powers, nor height, nor depth, nor anything else in all creation, will be able to separate us from the love of God in Christ Jesus our Lord' (Rom. 8: 38 f.). Outside Scripture this has hardly been better or more satisfyingly expressed than by Augustus Toplady in his magnificent hymn, 'A debtor to mercy alone'. What good reason we all have to sing, with him:

The work which His goodness began,
The arm of His strength will complete;
His promise is Yea and Amen,
And never was forfeited yet.
Things future, nor things that are now,
Nor all things below or above,
Can make Him His purpose forgo,
Or sever my soul from His love.

III SONSHIP

In the first two sections of his description of a Christian Paul has spoken for our assurance and comfort. Now he has a word to say about the greatness of our privilege, for the Christian is *a child of God* (verse 15). This reinforces all that has been said hitherto. For if we are children then we belong to the Family, and our possession of salvation is assured: we are the sons whom He has begotten by His own will (Jn. 1: 12; Jas. 1: 18), and whom, through His Son, He will bring to glory (Heb. 2: 10). Likewise, sons must necessarily share their Father's nature, and this is the meaning of the divine indwelling (Rom. 8: 9–17; 2 Pet. 1: 4). How differently God works from man! David had a son, Absalom, and nothing could obliterate that relationship. They were father and son even when they were also enemies—as David discovered too late and to his bitter sorrow (2 Sa. 18: 33). Yet David's forgiveness of one who was his son was belated, partial, and unreal (2 Sa. 14: 24). But we were never God's children at all. We were sinners, enemies (Rom. 5: 8,10), alienated (Col. 1: 21); yet when God forgave us He brought us right back, and not just to citizenship of His city, but membership of His family (Eph. 2: 18,19). Here is godlike forgiveness indeed!

IV LIGHT

The final item in the fourfold description stands in contrast to the other three. So far we have been dealing with hidden, personal truths. It is only known to God and the individual whether he truly possesses salvation; only God and the person concerned know if there is a reality of divine indwelling; only the Lord, who knows those who are His (2 Tim. 2: 19), and the individual know of the relationship of sonship. But the fourth element is one that any outsider can see and test. The Christian is to be a 'light', or better a 'lantern' or 'light-bearer' in the world (verse 15).

How practical Paul is! The privileges of being a Christian outnumber the responsibilities by three to one, but he will not allow us to savour the sweet satisfaction of sure salvation, divine indwelling, and family membership without facing us also and equally with the straight question: have you a clear testimony, as obvious and unmistakable as a lighthouse? And we dare not brush the question aside! We dare not lazily assume, as we are all too prone to do, that though this part of the description is not true of us yet the other three parts are! When David had no testimony it was because he was dislocated from God (Ps. 51:12–14). How can we say that we are right with God if we are falling down on the one *objective* test that Paul offers in these verses? Are we then lanterns? Does the light stream out from us? Praise God for all His benefits and privileges freely bestowed upon the redeemed—but there is another use for the mouth as well as that, and a 'crooked and perverse' world is waiting to hear from us. Our secrets are for sharing.

13 THE CONSEQUENCES OF SALVATION

GOD'S 'THEREFORE' IN VERSE 9 is matched by the Christian's 'therefore' in verse 12. That, in a nutshell, is what this passage is about. Just as God assessed the worth of His Son's life of obedience and reacted accordingly (verses 9–11), so the Christian must respond to the example of Christ (verses 12–18).

Before proceeding further, however, let us examine this connection a little more closely. If we go back to 2: 4, we recall that Paul is there teaching that in the last analysis the effective testimony of the church to the world depends upon the proper relationship of one individual to another within the church. It was at this point (2: 5) that he adduced the example of Christ. He is the great Model for all individual life, and His life of self-sacrificing obedience is the model for the believer who wants to live out the true assessment and aims displayed in 2: 3,4.

Paul is recalling all this when he writes 'therefore' in verse 12. He means, 'You have heard me call each individual of you to assess himself at his humble worth and to aim at the other man's good (2 : 3,4). You have followed me as I traced out the example of Christ in this (2: 5–8) and you have seen God's reaction to it (2: 9–11). Now let me tell you how you must react if the great example is to reappear in your lives.'

This, then, is the meaning of the opening word in verse 12. We are to learn from the Bible not only what is true but also how to respond to the truth. We are to learn from Paul not only what is the example of Christ but also how we are to respond to it so as to make it real in our lives. Christlikeness is the greatest possible concern of the Christian. Here is the procedure for attaining it.

1 WORK (*verses 12,13*)

It ought surely to take us somewhat by surprise that Paul says our first response to the example of Jesus is to *work*. Only a little while ago we understood Paul to say that all the work of salvation was God's. He initiated us into Christ, maintains us in Christ as He energizes both the will and the deed, and underwrites the outcome of the whole procedure. What then is there left for us to do, if indeed 'God is at work in you, both to will and to work for his good pleasure'? Logic says, 'Nothing! Let go and let God!' Scripture, however, says the reverse. It says, 'Work.' The same Scripture which underlines the completeness of the work of the indwelling God commands us that our necessary response is to 'work out your own salvation'. The person who is new-created in Christ is a worker (*cf.* Eph. 2: 10). The person who is concerned to be like Jesus must work. That is Paul's first command in the matter.

There are five marks of the working Christian. He is responsible, consecrated, accountable, confident, and obedient. First, then, we must work as those who are *responsible*. Paul says, 'Work out *your own* salvation.' The care of the individual soul is committed to the individual; responsibility for personal spiritual progress is committed to the person himself. This is not to say that Christians are to be exclusive individualists, or that no benefit accrues from the fellowship of the church. Nor is it to deny those Scriptures which enforce upon us mutual spiritual care and encouragement (*e.g.* Heb. 10: 24,25). But it is to exalt into a general principle for Christian living the command which Paul gave to the Ephesian elders, 'Take heed *to yourselves* and to all the flock' (Acts 20: 28); and to Timothy, 'Take heed *to yourself* and to your teaching' (1 Tim. 4: 16).

We are also to work for those who are *consecrated* to the task. This emphasis is expressed by the verb translated 'work', which implies 'to carry out to the full and to the end'. It is used in Ephesians 6: 13 of the soldier who has resolutely faced every foe, and fought to the end of the battle, and who, by his persistent, undaunted battling, remains, in Weymouth's memorable phrase, a 'victor on the field'. In exactly the same way, the apostle here calls us to the battle of sanctification, in which foes of every description must be encountered, and in which the fight continues till the end. It is a battle which calls for committed determination and consecrated perseverance. Salvation, perfectly accomplished by Christ and given by His grace to the Christian, must be carried out to the end and to the full.

A third facet of Paul's call to work, is that we must work as those who are *accountable*. He says, 'Work . . . with fear and trembling.' There is, of course, a sense in which fear has no place in the Christian's life. That is to say, salvation is his sure possession, and he need never fear that ultimately he could be lost, or that his salvation could be snatched from him (Jn. 10: 28). Our Saviour is too strong for that to happen, and our salvation is so completely secured by Him that already now, as God sees us, we are at His right hand in the heavenly places (Eph. 2: 5,6). Yet, on the other hand, there is a fear which the Christian loses at his peril, and that is 'godly fear, growing out of recognition of weakness and of the power of temptation; filial dread of offending God' (Vincent). It is not the terror of the lost sinner in the face of a Holy God, but the trembling reverence of the son before a loving, holy Father. It is the fear which urged Paul on to evangelize (2 Cor. 5: 11) knowing that he must render account before the judgment seat of Christ (2 Cor. 5: 9,10); it is that 'fear of God' which he urged upon the same Corinthians as a motive for the pursuit of holiness (2 Cor. 7: 1); it is the fear which, according to Peter, is the abiding feature of the life of one who knows God as Father (1 Pet. 1: 17). The loving Father, who spared not His only Son but freely gave Him up on our behalf, the Lord Jesus 'who gave himself for us to redeem us from all iniquity and to purify for himself a people of his own' (Tit. 2: 14)—These will call us to account, and should we not therefore tremble as we work, lest They be disappointed?

In the fourth place, we are to work as those who are *confident* of the outcome. The command is, 'Work . . . for God is at work in you, both to will and to work.' It is noticeable that he did not say, 'though it is God at work', as if to undervalue the consecrated activity of the Christian; nor does he say, 'just as God works in you', as if to set the two activities on a par. He says, 'Work . . . because God works.' The work to which the Christian is called is a work of possession or appropriation. The great indwelling God is constantly and effectually at work bringing about a willingness and eagerness to do His will, and a matching power of accomplishment. By the activity of 'work' the Christian makes these benefits his own. In the language of Obadiah (verse 17), he possesses his possessions. For this reason, in another setting, Paul asserts of himself that he fights 'not as uncertainly'. To be sure, the Christian must needs tremble as he contemplates the power of temptation; but what is that compared to the undergirding, all-accomplishing power of God? Here is the sure ground of confidence on which the Christian takes his stand for battle.

The final mark of the Christian's work is that it is *obedient*. We note this last of all, but for Paul it was first of all. The work to which the Christian is called is not a broad, undefined 'do-good-ism', nor is it, in the first instance, a series of skirmishes with temptation as and when it raises its head. It is the positive attempt to follow the Lord Jesus Christ in a life of unswerving obedience to God. See how Paul puts it, 'You have always obeyed, so now, . . . work. . . .' The work is the exercise of obedience toward God. This was the governing motive of Christ Himself in His great career of self-denial. He 'carried His obedience (to God) even as far as death itself' (see verse 8). Therefore the Christian must have obedience as his primary characteristic, 'Therefore . . . as you have always obeyed' (verse 12). Such obedience is an absolute requirement. It is not dependent upon other conditions being fulfilled. Indeed, it is irrespective of all other conditions. It is 'always . . . not only as in my presence but much more in my absence'. It was the one thing that God required of Adam in Eden (Gn. 2: 16,17); it was the primary requirement of God from His redeemed at Sinai (Ex. 20: 1 ff.). It is the first mark of the Christian: to know the word of God's command, and to obey it. In practical terms, this ought to be the motive and outcome of our daily Bible reading. It should be kept under the shelter of the constant prayer, 'What does my Lord bid His servant?', and constantly followed by obedience.

II CHARACTER (*verses 14,15*)

Following upon the response of work is the response of Christian *character*. Verse 14 opens up further the active life to which the Christian is called, 'Do all things'. But we find that the emphasis is not on the fact of being up and doing, nor on the things which must be done, but on the character which is to be displayed in every action. The emphasis, so to speak, is on the adverbial phrases, 'without grumbling or questioning . . .'; and upon the adjectival qualifications, 'blameless and innocent . . . without blemish'. The threefold grouping of these words displays the three spheres of Christian character: towards other people, in personal life and integrity, and in the sight of God.

Towards others, Christian character is shown by the absence of 'grumbling or questioning'. 'Grumbling' means selfish complaining (Mt. 20: 11), critical concentration on small points (Lk. 5: 30), impatience towards what is not at once understood (Jn. 6: 41), airing self-centred grievances (Acts 6: 1), and grudging unwillingness to be helpful (1 Pet. 4: 9). Throughout these examples the stress is on outward activity, and not every use of the noun and its related verb is necessarily improper. For example, the complaint of the widows in Acts 6: 1 was justifiable, but even here we can see the thinness of the ice, for nowhere does the self-centred heart of man more quickly take control than when it comes to the machinery of criticism and the promptings of self-interest.

By contrast, the word which is translated 'questionings' is inward in its main significance, and often appears as 'reasonings'. What the warning against 'grumblings' forbids in outward conduct, that against 'questionings' forbids as an inward attitude of heart and mind towards other people. The verb appears in this sense, for example, in Luke 3: 15, and 12: 17; the noun is translated 'thoughts' in Luke 2: 35, and 'questionings' in Luke 24: 38, and in all these cases it is the unexpressed thought of the heart that is intended.

In summary, then, Christian character is to be expressed in all our actions towards other people, and in all our thoughts about them. Both these words are in the plural, and the force of this may well be paraphrased, 'without carping, selfish criticisms *of any sort,* whether spoken or silent'.

Secondly, the Christian is to display evidence of his salvation by his own personal character—the man considered in and by himself. This again falls into two aspects, and as we consider them the requirement will become plainer. He is to be 'blameless and innocent'. The first word has reference to the comment another person might pass upon him, and the second to the comment he might pass on himself, knowing, as he does, his own inner life. 'Blameless' points to a life that is above reproach, above criticism. Just as, on the one hand, the Christian is not to give himself to carping criticism of other people, so, by the way he lives, he is to remove all cause of just criticism against himself. Does it matter, then, what others think of us? Certainly it does! We will never be without those who delight to make unjust accusations, and to take away our good name without cause—both Christians and non-Christians. That, however, is not the point. We cannot be held accountable for the malice or unkindness of others; but we are accountable for this, that no-one should have just ground for pointing the finger of condemnation at us.

It is possible, however, that a life may be publicly above reproach, and yet secretly vile. Once more, the Christian must learn to guard the hidden man of the heart. He must be 'innocent', that is 'unmixed' or 'pure' or 'sincere'. The commentators point out that the word is used, in secular contexts, of *undiluted* wine, or of metal *without alloy*. That is to say, the word describes something which retains its proper, professed nature through and through. So is the Christian to be: not a man who professes one thing outwardly, by life and lip, but secretly practises and desires another. He is to be of *unmixed* godliness of character. It was for this *wholly good* life that Paul was striving when he testified that he always took pains 'to have a clear conscience toward God and toward men' (Acts 24: 16). He urged Timothy to place the same importance upon a clear conscience by pointing to the shipwreck of those who failed to 'hold faith and a good conscience' (1 Tim. 1: 19).

The greatest test of Christian character comes last. What does God think of us? The Christian is to be 'without blemish'. This is the spotless life which God purposed for us, when He chose us before the foundation of the world and sent His Son to die for us (Eph. 1: 4); it describes what God will in the end accomplish when He presents to Himself a church 'without spot' (Eph. 5: 27); it is the word chosen to express the unblemished character of Christ (Heb. 9: 14; 1 Pet. 1: 19). It is the life which not even the holy God Himself can find ground to criticize. To this the Christian is called, as a consequence of salvation. Part of his possession, as he possesses salvation, is that by the will of God 'we have been sanctified through the offering of the body of Jesus Christ once for all' (Heb. 10: 10). This completely accomplished holiness must be appropriated outwardly and inwardly by that unremitting work of obedience to which the saved are called.

III TESTIMONY (*verses 15b,16a*)

This standard of Christian character is so lofty as to seem unreasonable. Does Paul mean us to take him seriously? It is evident that he does, for he ties his precepts right down to the facts of our daily circumstances. He does not say, 'Live like this in your imaginations'; nor, 'Live like this when you are among other Christians at conferences.' There is nothing either of idealistic fiddle-faddle or of unrealistic isolationism about Paul. He says that this threefold call to Christian character is to be worked out '*in the midst of* a crooked and perverse generation, *among whom* you shine as lights *in the world*'. It is in the 'brass tacks' of daily life that Christian character is to be displayed, making a stark contrast with the contemporary world which is described both as inwardly 'twisted' and outwardly 'perverted', or turned off course.

But a silent example, while it may impress, will never save. It needs explanation; it needs a 'word'. And the Christian is a light-bearer in the world, not only by his personal character, but also by means of 'the word of life'. But the order used by Paul is important. His first call is for quality of life and then for the spoken testimony. Life without word is an uninterpreted parable; word without life is idle gossip. It is only when he has first told Christians what they are (saved and indwelt by God, verses 12,13), and secondly called them to be what they are in terms of holiness (verses 14,15), that thirdly he summons them to talk (verse 16).

Their task as witnesses is described as 'holding fast the word of life'. The verb is ambiguous: it can mean either 'holding fast' (*i.e.*

the work of personal loyalty and obedience to the Word of God) or 'holding forth' (*i.e.* the work of biblical witnessing). Is it fair to ask for both meanings? After all, the ambiguity must have been equally clear to Paul, but he was content to leave it there. In any event, the double truth does no more than reinforce what the rest of the verses have been stressing: obedience to God is the only sound basis for testimony to the world; only those who 'hold fast' to the Word in their own lives can profitably 'hold forth' the word to others. Testimony ought to be considered inseparable from obedience, and obedience should be held as the priority task.

In the task of moving towards the world, the Christian has an armoury of one weapon, 'the word of life'. Here is the ground of confidence, even when faced with a 'crooked and perverse', a twisted and perverted, generation, for it is not only a word which is concerned with life but a word which gives the life of which it speaks; it 'has in itself a principle as well as a message of life' (Vincent)—and we are given no other tool, for none other is required. The Christian goes to the world not saying 'I think', nor even 'the church teaches', but only 'the Word of God says'.

IV ENCOURAGEMENT (*verses 16b–18*)

This, then, is the life of Christ-likeness: a life of work, character, and testimony. But the Lord Jesus had the encouragement of the 'joy that was set before him' (Heb. 12: 2), and Paul does not leave us without encouragement as we pursue the goal of being like our Saviour.

First, he encourages us by showing the intrinsic worth of the sort of life he has outlined. He speaks of it as the 'sacrificial offering of your faith' (verse 17). The word 'offering' points to our status and function as 'priests' (1 Pet. 2: 5,9; Rev. 1: 6). We have no animal oblations to make such as occupied the priests of the old covenant, but we have nevertheless a 'sacrifice', just as much appointed by God and acceptable to Him (*cf.* Eph. 5: 1 f.) as ever theirs was. Our sacrifice, to which we are prompted by our faith, is this life of obedience, and character-building, and holiness and witness. This is its intrinsic worth. It is our priestly service to God.

Secondly, Paul encourages us in following Christ by expressing his intense apostolic approval of this sort of life. He has a characteristically forceful way of putting this in verse 17. We must remember that his imminent death was at this time a distinct possibility (1: 19 ff.). He speaks of it here as his being 'poured as a libation'. The word refers to the 'drink offering' of the Old Testament. The regulations for this part of the sacrificial system are not absolutely clear, but we can at least say that the drink offering was the accompaniment of a larger sacrifice; it was the small thing which brought a major offering to completeness (*e.g.* Nu. 15: 8 ff.). Paul says that he would count it nothing but joy that he had 'laboured to weariness' (for this is what the word means in verse 16) if by this means he can 'put the finishing touch' to their appointed sacrifice of work, character, and testimony. He could hardly have rated more highly the life to which he calls them.

But he has, none the less, a still higher value to express. For, thirdly, he encourages us on our way by showing that the life of Christ-imitation is acceptable before Christ Himself in the day of His coming. Paul looks forward to the joy that will be his when Christ returns (verse 16) if only his Philippians have held on to the course which he has outlined for them. Could he so rejoice if Christ had to rebuke them at His return, if there was no 'well done' (Mt. 25: 21; Lk. 19: 17)? But what joy will be his if and when he beholds Christ's favour towards them and approval of them! And the road towards that day and to a joyful standing before Christ at His appearing is this road of obedient work, patient pursuit of a holy character, and shining testimony to a dark world.

14 MODEL CHRISTIANS (1)

IN THE WONDERFUL VARIETY OF THE BIBLE, we come from the deep and reverent picture of the Lord Jesus Christ with which the chapter opened to this homely picture of three outstanding Christians, with which it closes. There is Paul, the writer, who by implication discloses himself, and there are Timothy and Epaphroditus whose characters he sketches as he commends them to the church at Philippi. But the two ends of the chapter, though contrasting, are not unconnected. The things which Paul was inspired to imply concerning himself and to state concerning the others show them as three men who have taken the example of the Lord Jesus seriously. He so consecrated Himself in obedient service to God that He poured Himself out for the benefit of others. They so consecrated themselves to God that self was subdued in the service of other Christians. He is the Christian's Model. They are model Christians.

We have in these verses a veritable window into the heart of Paul. We know from other scriptures that when required to do so he could assert and enforce all the authority that was his as an apostle of Christ. If people challenged his right to be called an apostle, they were soon made to realize that on this point Paul would brook no contradiction, and no loss of authority. His rebuke to the Corinthians is clear, 'Am I not an apostle? Have I not seen Jesus our Lord?' (1 Cor. 9: 1). The Galatians likewise found that Paul could insist on his apostolic status, 'Paul an apostle—not from men nor through man, but through Jesus Christ and God the Father' (Gal. 1: 1). However, returning to

Philippians, we find, not a different Paul, but another facet of the same Paul. We discover that his proper dignity and authority as an apostle who could always 'magnify (his) ministry' (Rom. 11: 13), is entirely divorced from any haughtiness or self-assertiveness of personal character. The two things went together in Paul's life, in a completely harmonious personality: the dignity and exaltation of office, and the humility and self-forgetfulness of one who modelled himself upon Jesus Christ (1 Cor. 11: 1).

One turn of phrase in verse 22 reveals this perfectly. Paul is speaking of Timothy, and offering proof of his excellence as a Christian. They are like father and son together. If we could close our eyes for a moment to what we know is written in this verse, and try to predict what the parallelism requires, it would come out like this, 'as a son serves a father, so he served me'. They were father and son together. The one was the natural leader, the other the natural subordinate. But Paul does not say, 'so he served me'. To do this would be to exalt himself, to make himself a man to whom others ought to be subordinate. He says instead, 'so he served with me'. We were 'co-slaves'.

The idea of 'slavery' introduces, and at the same time sums up, Paul's attitude towards the Lord Jesus Christ. His attitude was the slave's attitude of total submission. It is displayed in this passage in two special spheres. First, Paul was submissive in the matter of the Lord's ordering of his life. Concerning the proposed mission of Timothy (verse 19), he expresses 'hope in the Lord Jesus'; and in verse 24, concerning his own future, he expresses 'trust in the Lord'. One is a comparatively small matter—whether Timothy can go or not—the other is comparatively much more important—whether Paul lives or dies, whether he lives as a prisoner or as a free man. Each alike is resigned to the Lord's overruling. The extent of Paul's submission to the will of the Lord is specially seen in the second matter. Once more may we try to imagine what Paul might have said here? 'I trust in the justice of Roman Law that I shall be released, for after all there is no real charge against me'; or, 'I trust in my position as a Roman citizen.' But he says neither of these. From the Roman court, he appeals away to the highest court of all, the throne of God; from any assertion of personal prestige, he resigns to the authority of his Lord. Paul's *doctrine* taught him that a sovereign

God ruled all things: whether freedom or imprisonment, comfort or discomfort, sickness or health. The child of God lives under the sovereignty of God. Paul's *practice* was to accept without question or rebellion what the Lord ordained. The same Lord who called him to be an apostle could and would also ordain the sphere of apostleship, be it a free-roving commission to the Gentile world, or the restrictive limits of a Roman gaol.

Secondly, Paul was submissive to the Lord in the matter of service. Submission did not carry the implications of inactivity; it was the submissiveness of perfect obedience. Along with Timothy, Paul 'slaved in the furtherance of the gospel'. Notice how this points to Paul as modelling himself upon the Lord Jesus, who took 'the form of a slave' (verse 7, mg.). Those who are His must accept His pattern. Paul did not rest in gospel privileges and leave it at that; he was a slave for the gospel. Paul did not play with the gospel, working with it as a man follows a hobby; he was a slave for the gospel. Here we learn the extent of submission which the Lord seeks in His followers—the total capitulation to His authority which the word 'slave' implies. We learn also the manner in which this submission works out in practice: the subduing of every capacity, talent, and energy to promoting *the gospel*. This is the normative form of Christian slavery. To submit to the Lord is to devote every faculty to the spread of the gospel of the Lord.

Now, in the case of the Lord Jesus, He took the form of a slave in order to pour Himself out for the good of others. If Paul followed Him in the matter of slavery, did he also copy Him in his regard for other people? What was Paul's attitude towards others? The present passage tells us of his attitude towards other Christians, and it is good that we should dwell on it. For (so it seems) it is exceedingly easy to be devoted to the work of Christ, the spread of the gospel, and the winning of the outsider, and yet to fall down tragically in the matter of relationships with other Christians.

We can discern three features of Paul's attitude towards other Christians. In the first place, he saw them as *worthy of the best he had to give*. Of Timothy, Paul said that there was no-one like him (verse 20). Timothy was in a class by himself. Yet it was Timothy whom Paul proposed to give to the Philippian church.

Of Epaphroditus, Paul urged that he was worthy of signal honour (verse 29) and could be described only in terms of the highest praise (verse 25). Yet Paul gladly sent Epaphroditus back to Philippi to serve the needs of the church there. Just like the Lord Jesus! He possessed the shared glories of heaven, but He gave them up (*cf.* 2 Cor. 8: 9); He possessed a unique, immortal nature, but He submitted to death. Paul also gave the best he had for other Christians.

Secondly, other Christians called forth *his warm affection and ungrudging praise*. Timothy was like his own child (verse 22), and Epaphroditus was one whose death would have been an almost unbearable loss (verse 27). Nothing could show more perfectly the way in which the grace of God can transform a man's affections. For Paul was born the exclusive Jew, and grew up the proud Pharisee (3: 5). Yet here he is embracing as a son the 'mongrel' Timothy (Acts 16: 1), and living in perfect brotherhood with the Gentile 'dog' Epaphroditus! What a rebuke to our lack of love towards our fellow Christians! And Paul's love for them, as here, was no lukewarm or merely conventional thing. This is shown in the full and generous praise which he bestows. The verses in question (verses 20–22, 25–29) will occupy us in more detail presently, so we need not dwell on them now, saving to read them thoughtfully and to discern the loving heart which prompted them. Here is true Christian generosity: to reckon Timothy's service the equal of his own (verse 22); to commend Epaphroditus to the praise and honour of the church, not alarmed lest his own praise and honour from that quarter should be diminished, or the limelight captured by somebody else.

Finally, other Christians were *the object of Paul's personal concern*. Paul 'thought it necessary' (verse 25) to send Epaphroditus to Philippi. This was not simply because Epaphroditus was becoming restive and distracted in mind, knowing that the Philippians were worried about him, but because Paul himself was restless and anxious, and could himself find no relaxation of spirit until their fears and anxieties were allayed. He purposed by the return of their messenger that 'you may rejoice . . . and that *I may be less anxious*' (verse 28). Although he dreaded the 'sorrow upon sorrow' which would have been caused had

Epaphroditus died (verse 27) he is none the less ready to lose Epaphroditus in order to secure the greater well-being of the Philippian church. His 'being cheered' is a by-product of their 'welfare' (verse 19).

Paul is presently to exhort us to 'join in imitating me' (3: 17). His unwitting self-portrait is clear: deep, personal humility, resting upon submission to the Lord and submissive—though exceedingly energetic—obedience in His cause, and issuing in the subordination of personal interests to those of other Christians; and that is not in a cold, or 'merely' dutiful way, but because the grace of God had changed his heart so that he loved them. The Lord Jesus Christ is the Christian's Model; Paul was a model Christian.

PHILIPPIANS 2: 19–30

15 MODEL CHRISTIANS (2)

WE TURN NOW FROM THE INCIDENTAL PORTRAIT of Paul himself to the deliberate 'thumb-nail' sketches which he offers us of his two choice fellow-workers, Timothy and Epaphroditus. Here again the homely narrative is in striking contrast with the theological heights of the portrayal of the Lord Jesus, but the continuity of the two sections in their spirit is clear. Once again the Great Exemplar is followed by two men whose consecration to God issued in their service to the people of God.

First for consideration comes Timothy the Pre-eminent (verses 19–22). There is no-one 'like him' (verse 20). The precise intention of this description is not easy to decide, and the commentators are by no means agreed. Three possibilities, each equally suitable, arise: in the first place, the word may refer to the personal uniqueness of Timothy, 'I have no-one who is quite like him.' This suits the context, in that Paul proceeds almost at once to bring Timothy into contrast with 'all' (verse 21) who 'look after their own interests'. However, the word may equally refer to the apostolic approval of Timothy, 'I have no-one else who is so like me.' This also is agreeable to the context, for Paul goes on to describe that oneness and unanimity which exists between the two of them as a father-son relationship (verse 22), which gives Timothy his unique place in the apostolic regard (*cf.* 1 Tim. 1: 2,18; 2 Tim. 1: 2; 2: 1). Or again Paul may have intended to refer to Timothy's special suitability for the proposed task, 'I have no-one else equal to the task.' And once more this meaning fits the passage, for the words which follow immediately relate Timothy's unique capacity to the Philippian situation with which he is to deal: he will 'be genuinely anxious for your welfare'. It is surely likely, as we have said before, that if a word seems so obviously ambiguous to us, Paul was aware of this, and content with the ambiguity. It is as though he was saying to us: here is a man who is in every way a pre-eminent Christian. As regards his personal qualities, the needs of the work, and apostolic approval, Timothy stands out from all others. We will, then, be all the more anxious clearly to see the marks of this outstanding man. What makes a Christian pre-eminent?

The first characteristic of the pre-eminent Timothy is that he possessed *a native, genuine, painstaking care for other Christians.* He will be 'naturally and genuinely painstaking' as we might translate the latter part of verse 20. Lightfoot comments on the word which the RSV gives as 'genuinely', 'as a birthright, as an instinct derived from his spiritual parentage'. Vincent writes, 'naturally, by birth-relation, and therefore truly or genuinely'. There is nothing forced or artificial about Timothy's concern; it is the genuine product of a regenerate nature. And it expresses itself vigorously and determinedly, for the verb 'be anxious' is that which found culpable expression in the harassed anxiety of Martha (Lk. 10: 41), but which is a necessary feature of apostolic pastoral concern (2 Cor. 11: 28).

The second feature of his outstanding companion which Paul underlines is that he *outstrips all in his devotion to the Lord Jesus Christ.* The 'all' of verse 21 must be taken as a broad generalization. For example, it must necessarily exclude Epaphroditus, who plainly put Jesus first (verse 30). But what a sad and condemning generalization it is that Paul should find the one common feature of the general run of Christians to be that self-seeking spirit which degrades Jesus Christ to second place! It was not so with Timothy: the things of Jesus Christ were his top priority.

The third mark of Timothy's character was *his ungrudging willingness to accept the position God gave him.* 'As a son with a father he has served with me.' Paul may soften the relationship by the gentle and understanding words 'with me', putting himself on the same level as Timothy in the slavery of the gospel, but none the less the truth of Timothy's subordinate place is clear. He was not only a slave of the gospel, but, so to speak, a second-class slave! It was his task to be a lieutenant, a second-in-command. And he was ready that it should be so. He never usurped.

The fourth feature is implicit in what has just been said, but may be mentioned for completeness. Timothy was *a slave for the furtherance of the gospel*. He, with Paul, stands in the succession of Him who took 'the form of a slave'. He was a person whose whole life was given to the gospel; who asserted no personal claims against, or to the detriment of, the gospel; but who accepted and obeyed its total claim upon himself.

But these four aspects of Timothy are not simply four separate items. They are one whole, and the passage makes them identical. Verses 20,21, by the parallelism involved, equate being 'genuinely anxious for your welfare' with 'looking after the interests of Jesus Christ'. Let us try to make this clear by a free paraphrase of the verses: 'Timothy is outstanding, and will show it by the way he will care for you. This distinguishes him from the generality of Christians, who seek their own good, and not the things of Jesus Christ.' Putting this positively, a Christian displays his pre-eminent devotion to the Lord Jesus by seeking the true welfare of others. It is necessarily so, for the Lord Jesus displayed His total obedience to God by pouring Himself out wholly for others. Had He not done so, His consecration would have remained theoretical, if not hypothetical. Timothy was like his Lord.

In the same way verses 21 and 22 are linked together. The facts mentioned in verse 22 are the proof of the position adopted in verse 21. Let us follow the sequence again by means of a paraphrase: 'Do you wish to have proof of Timothy's pre-eminent devotion to the Lord Jesus? Here it is: he slaved in the furtherance of the gospel.' Thus, just as verses 20,21 identified seeking the good of other Christians with giving the prior place to the interests of Jesus Christ, so verses 21,22 identify giving the prior place to the Lord Jesus with being a slave for the gospel's sake. And this, in consequence, is the portrait of the pre-eminent Christian, cast in the apostolic mould and useful for the work. He puts the Lord first by seeking the spiritual good of others through a sacrificial gospel ministry.

The third model Christian is Epaphroditus the Praiseworthy.

'Honour such men', says Paul (verse 29). What makes a Christian *honourable*? The answer is bound to seem repetitive. We find the same lessons over again. Let us be clear that this is the purpose of the Holy Spirit. Scripture does not repeat truth for the sake of filling up space, but to give it emphasis. And so now, for the third time, we are to be brought face to face with a man in whom the example of Jesus Christ shines, a man whose consecrated devotion to Christ was displayed in service of other Christians and in the cause of the gospel.

In relation to other Christians Epaphroditus was marked out by the fellowship he offered to them, by the placing of his gifts at the disposal of the church, and by his concern for their good. Paul found him a 'brother and *fellow* worker and *fellow* soldier'. We do not wish to snatch at small indications of character and magnify them into something Paul did not intend, but, none the less, these three descriptions point to a man of harmonious disposition. Had he been a quarrelsome, nagging, restless person, ready to pick out faults and quick to criticize, he might still, in Christian charity, have been called a worker, and a soldier, but he would not have been awarded a bar to his medal, 'fellow worker, fellow soldier'.

Then, again, he was the one the church singled out as their messenger, and Paul commends him for the way he discharged his task. He was 'your messenger' (verse 25), the one who brought their service towards the apostle to completeness (verse 30). We will dwell presently on the whole-hearted way he accomplished his service, 'risking his life to complete your service to me'. That phrase teaches us much about the man, but here it shows specially that he did not grudge to place his gifts at the disposal of the local church. In the group of Christians with which he was associated, he had the name for being trustworthy and willing. They were content to commit their trust to him, and he was ready to carry it out.

But he carried out this work in a very personal manner. It was not just a job to be done. He was personally implicated in it by the way he went about it. He almost lost his life in his zeal to minister on the Philippians' behalf to Paul (verse 30), and this warm-hearted, self-forgetful regard for other Christians made him almost demented (verse 26, 'distressed' literally has this meaning) when he learned that they were anxious about him! Far from feeling gratified that he was the centre of attention, something of a popular figure in the home church, it drove him to mental and spiritual torment to consider that he was the cause of worry to them.

Behind and throughout this description of Epaphroditus' great record of devotion to others, there is seen his fundamental consecration to the Lord Jesus. In Christian service he was no passenger, but a *worker* and a *soldier,* emphasizing now the nouns themselves rather than the prefixes to them. Here the related ideas of effort, endurance, and loyalty are grouped together: the effort of Christian work; the endurance to keep it up and to fight to the end; the loyalty of the good soldier who keeps himself free from worldly entanglements in order to please Him who called him as a soldier (2 Tim. 2: 3,4). This is all summed up in one word, which sets before us a glorious picture and definition of consecrated living, 'for he nearly died for the work of Christ, risking his life' (verse 30). The phrase 'unto death' is identical to that used of the Lord Himself in verse 8, who carried His obedience 'unto death'. Epaphroditus was following in the great succession. But the manner in which he did it tells more of the man. He 'threw down his life like a gambler's stake'. Put it another way—though the gambling metaphor catches the meaning of the Greek—he took a calculated risk, involving the expenditure of all he had, relying only on the trustworthiness of Jesus Christ. He staked all on Jesus, knowing that He could not fail.

Says Paul, 'Honour such men.' Well might we honour such a man; and well might we wish to be like him. Indeed, that is the purpose of the portraiture, not only of Epaphroditus but also of Timothy, and indeed of Paul himself. Here is the grace of God effectually at work in three varied characters, coming from varied backgrounds, but all one in Christ Jesus. Here is the effectual working of the indwelling God in three of His redeemed. What was true of them can be true of us; God has not changed!

16 RELIGIOUS BUT REJOICING

IS IT JUSTIFIABLE FOR A CHRISTIAN to be angry? Is controversy and argument a permitted activity for Christians? We can be, by fits and starts, both unduly sensitive and culpably insensitive on these matters. On the one side differences of opinion are regarded as a blot upon 'the fellowship' and therefore ought to be suppressed; and on the whole it is this attitude which prevails in the majority of Christians, and much offence is taken if any suspicion of heat enters into our discussions. On the other hand, there are those who pride themselves on 'speaking their mind', and whose virtuous regard for truth is often indulged to the detriment of the 'affection and sympathy' which should characterize the new nature of the regenerate man.

Speaking broadly on this topic we see in the New Testament that there is a justifiable anger, but that its display is hedged about with warnings. James (1: 19 f.) does not place a final bar to anger when he says 'let every man be slow to anger', but he hastens to warn that 'the anger of man does not work the righteousness of God'. Likewise, Paul, in a passage which dwells notably upon sins of speech and the need to eradicate them (Eph. 4: 25 ff.), admits that anger has a place in the life of the Christian: 'Be angry.' But how swiftly he adds 'but do not sin; do not let the sun go down on your anger'. It is as though he was erecting a warning sign at the entrance to a dangerous path. Anger is always trembling on the verge of sinfulness.

Yet Paul often shows himself as an angry and controversial man, and his example is worth more extended study than we can pause to make here. We must raise only the one matter which is inseparable from our understanding of this present passage in Philippians. One thing never failed to rouse the apostle's wrath and to fire him for controversy; and that was when what he himself called 'the truth of the gospel' (Gal. 2: 14) was at stake. We are not to assume that nothing else made him angry or that this was the only point on which he felt controversy was justifiable; it just happens that it is the matter which is now relevant. The extent of his indignation can be measured by the word 'accursed' as used against those who preach 'a gospel contrary to that which you received' (Gal. 1: 9). The importance which he attached to entering the lists in defence of this gospel is shown by his opposition even to Peter on this very point. He says, 'I opposed him to his face' (Gal. 2: 11), thereby showing not only that in the cause of the truth there can be no respect of persons, but also setting the pattern for Christian controversy —no back-door tittle-tattle, no smear campaigns, no secondhand dealing, but straightforward, manly encounter, person to person, and in the presence of witnesses (Gal. 2: 14). 'The truth of the gospel' must be known, asserted, defended, and its opposite rejected, opposed and denounced. We have no apostolic warrant for any other course.

It is exactly this which introduces very explosive material into the opening verses of Philippians 3. What words he uses: 'Look out for . . . dogs . . . evil-workers . . .'! So surprising are they, and so great is the contrast with the gentle and joyous language which characterizes this Epistle, that some commentators urge that having begun on what we call 'Chapter 3' Paul was interrupted by news that old opponents of the gospel were active at Philippi and he wrathfully breaks off his thought to smite them hip and thigh. The hypothesis rests upon the correct observation of unexpected wrath in verse 2, but none the less it is not necessary. Indeed it is hardly even likely, for if the topic on which he launched in verses 1,2 was so unsuited to the topic which he has in mind in verse 3 we might reasonably suppose that the apostle would have been the first to recognize the incongruity and to provide some harmonizing introduction. But the matter can be explained smoothly and in sequence.

The word translated 'finally' ought to be understood as, 'To proceed, then. . . .' It is doubtful if the meaning 'finally' is required by any of the places where the word occurs in the New Testament, and it is certainly misleading here. Basically the word means 'the remainder', and it is often used with the meaning 'henceforth' or 'for the future' (*e.g.* Acts 27: 20; 1 Cor. 7: 29, 2 Tim. 4: 8). This meaning would be very suitable here. Paul sums up his teaching so far with a command, 'Henceforth, rejoice in the Lord.' Without vitally altering this view of the connection with what has gone before, it is better, however, to translate in a way which indicates that Paul is resuming his main line of teaching. Thus 2: 17 f. dwelt on the topic of joy, but the main concern was the mutual joy of Christians with each other. Paul is not content with this as a final word about Christian joy, and so, having digressed slightly to speak of his plans for Timothy and Epaphroditus, he now picks up the main threads again: 'To proceed then, brethren. . . .'

The command he now gives is a suitable conclusion to what has gone before and introduction to what follows. This is a most Christ-glorifying Epistle. The Lord Jesus has been shown as the ground of our salvation (1: 1) and its guarantor (1: 6), the means of fruitfulness (1: 11), the Christian's message (1: 15 ff.), his absorbing interest (1: 20 ff.) and supreme example (2: 5 ff.). In what follows in chapter three Paul displays the Lord Jesus as the Christian's pride (verse 3), his choicest possession (verse 7), the object of his ambition (verse 8), his pattern (verse 10), his loyalty (verse 12), his crucified and coming Saviour (verses 18,20). Since this Christ-centred teaching will occupy us in detail in our final study we will elaborate it no further here, but enough has been shown to justify the assertion that the command, 'Rejoice in the Lord' stands as a watershed in the Epistle, for it is a command which emphatically focuses all upon Him.

How then shall we understand it? A parallel phrase used earlier will help. In 1: 18 Paul wrote 'in that (*i.e.* in the preaching of Christ) I rejoice'. What did he mean? He meant, 'It is this which makes me happy—this, and not that all think well of me, or that I should be released.' He meant, 'It is in this that I find joy', or 'This is my joy.' Likewise, when he commands, 'Rejoice in the Lord', he intends, 'Let the Lord and Him alone make you happy', 'Find your joy in the Lord and in Him alone.'

The remainder of the chapter, as we shall see, can be understood as revealing the secrets of this joyous life, but our immediate task is to understand the first of them. It is this: if we are to rejoice in the Lord then we must be certain that we are holding and practising the true religion. Paul lays considerable emphasis on the importance of this teaching. Not only does he place it first, but (verse 1) he has previously dwelt on it, and he sees in it something that will be for the 'safety' of the Philippians. 'I do not find it irksome to return to old topics with you, indeed your safety requires it.' There are, in fact, three items which he says he is reiterating: a *warning,* 'Look out', an *assurance,* 'for we are . . .', and a *definition,* 'who worship . . . glory . . . put no confidence'. It will aid our understanding if we take them in a different order.

1 AN ASSURANCE (*verse 3a*)

It is striking that Paul, the great opponent of the retention of circumcision for Christians (*cf.* Acts 15), should choose this particular way of asserting his assurance that he and the Philippians were in the right as against those whom he calls 'the dogs'. '*We*', he says, with deliberate emphasis, 'are the true circumcision.' He could not have chosen a more suitable, biblical, or instructive word.

In the first place, he meant that 'we are the covenant people of God', for circumcision was introduced into Abraham's family, and thence passed to the whole Israelite nation as a mark of the special relationship which God had established with them. It marked the covenant people (*cf.* Jdg. 14: 3). This idea of a 'covenant' is the greatest of the unifying themes of the Bible. It is mentioned first to Noah (Gn. 6: 18) as that which preserves him from the calamity which overwhelmed his contemporaries. It comes to fuller flower in the dealing of God with Abram (Gn. 15: 18) when we are permitted to see that the covenant rests upon a sacrifice which God appoints (Gn. 15: 9–17). It is embodied in the sign of circumcision (Gn. 17: 10 ff.) and is the basis on which God was moved to save His people from Egypt (Ex. 2: 24; 6: 2–8). It reaches its fullest flowering through Moses and the redemption from Egypt, for it is specifically the people who were redeemed by the blood of the Lamb (Ex. 12) upon whom God bestows covenant status and seals the relationship with blood at Mount Sinai (Ex. 24: 4–8).

The covenant became the basis of prophetic predictions of the glorious future of God's people. Isaiah foretold an eternal 'covenant' of peace' (54: 10) wrought by the Servant of the Lord upon whom 'the chastisement of our peace' was laid (53: 5). Jeremiah looked forward to a 'new covenant' resting upon such a settlement of the sin-problem that God says 'I will forgive their iniquity, and I will remember their sin no more' (31: 31–34). Ezekiel saw that there would come 'a covenant of peace . . . an everlasting covenant' of which the central blessing would be the eternal dwelling of God in the midst of His people (37: 26–28) with universal implications. The Lord Jesus brought this glorious sequence of prophecies to its appointed climax: 'on the night when he was betrayed (he) took bread, and when he had given thanks, he broke it, and said, "This is my body which is for you. Do this in remembrance of me." In the same way also the cup, after supper, saying, "This cup is the new covenant in my blood . . ." ' (1 Cor. 11: 23–25; *cf.* Mt. 26: 28; Mk. 14: 24; Lk. 22: 20).

When Paul says 'we are the circumcision' he is claiming for himself and the Philippians the incredible privilege of being the undoubted heirs of this agelong divine programme of salvation. But there is something more to it even than that, for Paul does not simply say, 'we are the covenant people'. He says, 'We are the true circumcision.' What precisely does this imply? What is the relation of the sign of circumcision to the covenant itself? The key passage is Genesis 17, and the important point can be simply expressed. The covenant is God's promise. He goes on oath in certain specific matters. Abram is the recipient of the promise which is first personal: Abram becomes Abraham (verse 5), a vivid promise of regeneration or a new nature, for with the new name there is created a new man; secondly, national, a multitude of nations (verses 5b,6); thirdly, spiritual, 'to be God to you and to your descendants after you' (verse 7); fourthly, territorial, the 'land of your sojournings' (verse 8); and finally, by way of emphasizing the most important point, spiritual again, 'and I will be their God' (verse 8).

But Genesis 17 also defines the covenant in a second way. We read in verse 10, 'This is my covenant . . . you shall be circumcised.' The covenant which is first (verses 4–8) a promise of God made to a chosen man cannot suddenly change its nature, and when it is secondly (verses 10–14) defined in terms of an appointed sign it must still speak of a movement of grace from God to man. It can be stated in this way: circumcision symbolizes the application of the covenant promises of God to chosen individuals whom God has appointed to be the recipients of them.

What then does Paul mean when he says that 'we are the true circumcision'? He thinks of himself and his friends at Philippi as individually chosen by God to be the recipients of the promises of grace. And of what promise in particular? We saw that Genesis 17 stressed one aspect of the divine oath-taking: the promise of a spiritual relationship between God and Abraham, and thereafter the seed of Abraham. This promise became the biblical definition of the essence of the divine covenant, and in its classical formulation it stated, 'You shall be my people and I will be your God.' In this form it is the most quoted verse in the Bible and is found throughout (*e.g.* Dt. 29: 13; 2 Sa. 7: 24; Je. 31: 1,33; 32: 38; Ezk. 36: 28; 37: 27; 2 Cor. 6: 16; Heb. 8: 10; Rev. 21: 3). Paul's claim, then, for himself and the Philippians is quite explicit. They are the chosen people of God, individually born again, individually and collectively the heirs of that divine purpose of grace which has been the centrepiece of world history. It is as though he said to them, 'We may be absolutely assured that God has set His personal seal of choice and ownership and blessing upon us, for we are the true circumcision.'

II A DEFINITION (*verse 3*)

The glorious assurance of membership of God's chosen people and of possession of His promised blessings is too important to be a mere matter of personal intuition or wishful thinking, and, consequently, lest his first readers, or we, his later readers, should be deceived by an unfounded confidence in such a vital matter, Paul adds, in three defining clauses, the marks of membership: the experience of the Spirit of God, the attitude towards Jesus Christ, and the refusal of self-reliance. Here are the *upward, outward,* and *inward* aspects of true religion, for the Christian must always be attentive on three fronts: to be at one with God, to behave correctly towards and before his fellow men, and to guard his own inner life.

The upward aspect of true religion is that it is prompted and controlled by God's Spirit, '. . . worship by the Spirit of God' (RSV mg., *cf.* RV). The word 'worship', both as noun and verb, as it is used in the New Testament has an exclusively religious significance, and it holds together the two aspects of the word 'service' in our common usage. We speak of 'Christian service', but we also say 'Are you coming to the service today?' This conjunction of worship and work is interesting, and should immediately warn us not to make an unnatural and unbiblical separation between what happens inside and outside our church meetings. All our life is worship. Prayer is worship (Lk. 2: 37), and so is the consecrated life of a body presented to God (Rom. 12: 1). Worship involves the condition of the inner life (Lk. 1: 74; 2 Tim. 1: 3). It must be carried on with a correct attitude towards God (Heb. 12: 28) and it requires enabling from above (Heb. 12: 28).

All this is catered for by the words 'by the Spirit of God'. There is the touch of the supernatural upon the worship of those 'who by the inward presence of the consecrating and transforming Spirit offer the sacrifice not of dead victims but of a devoted and renewed life' (Vaughan). Worshipping by the Spirit of God delivers from bondage to any special place of worship, as if there and nowhere else could God be found (Jn. 4: 21–24). Worshipping by the Spirit of God delivers from the burden of obligatory animal oblations (Heb. 10: 15–18). Worshipping by the Spirit of God demands a heart that is right with Him (Rom. 1: 9), a body that is a fit temple for the Holy Ghost (1 Cor. 6: 19). But worshipping by the Spirit of God also speaks of the agency of that divine Spirit, at work in us, at prayer for us (Rom. 8: 26 f.), empowering worship acceptable to God. Worship is a holy thing, and it is also to be a thing of the deepest and most satisfying reality, for we have here the promise that in worship we are acceptable to God as His priestly servants through the operation of His Spirit (*cf.* Eph. 2: 18).

The outward mark of the people of God is that they 'glory in Christ Jesus'. If we give this word more vigorous translation the meaning will be plainer, 'boast about Christ Jesus'. He is their divine Obsession, the central concern of a one-track mind and a one-theme tongue. It bespeaks a complete satisfaction in Him, an overmastering appreciation of what He has done (Gal. 6: 14; 1 Cor. 2: 2), and an unremitting presentation of Him to the world as worthy of all praise. At the centre of the three characteristics of the people of God there is the One who alone is worthy to be central—for is He not the centre of all heaven (Rev. 5: 6; 7: 17)?—the Lord Jesus Christ.

Thus God has reached down from heaven to take a people for Himself. He has animated them into new life by His Spirit; He has displayed before them the beauty and satisfactoriness of His Son, and granted them belief in Him and love towards Him. But in doing this, He has displayed to them also what they are themselves, and, alongside the truth of the life-giving Spirit and the atoning Son, they must also confess the total absence of personal worth: they 'put no confidence in the flesh'. The spirit of self-satisfaction, self-glorification, and self-reliance is outlawed.

This is but the negative counterpart of the two great positives which have occupied our attention. If it is true that God's people are only reckoned such because the Spirit of God has quickened them from the death of trespasses and sins (Eph. 2: 1), what ground is there for self-satisfaction? If Jesus alone is fit to be boasted of, where is self-glorification? If the energy of the flesh can only speed a man on his way to hell (Eph. 2: 2,3), of what use is self-reliance? We shall see presently how seriously Paul took this abandonment of confidence in the flesh, and what in detail he meant by it. For the moment, in order that we may in principle learn to fear it, to flee from it, and to destroy it we simply note that it is a co-equal article of the Christian's Creed. 'I believe in the Holy Ghost who has given me new life, made me a priest of God, and who leads me in living worship. I believe in Jesus Christ who is the only Saviour and the only worthy Subject of adoring praise. And I believe that in me, that is to say, in my flesh, there dwells no good thing' (Rom. 7: 18).

III A WARNING (*verse 2*)

The first root of joy, then, is in true religion. But Paul, as a careful pastor, knows that it is not enough to declare the truth; it must also be hedged about with the denial of error. Therefore he erects a warning sign, 'Beware.' The word 'dogs' (*cf.* Dt. 23: 18; Ps. 22: 16; Mt. 7: 6; 15: 26; Rev. 22: 15) is as insulting as could be found, and no doubt was as offensive in Paul's day as it seems in the anti-controversialist atmosphere of our own. Yet Paul does not hesitate to use it, which indicates that something crucial was involved, for such a word is not adopted lightly.

The point at issue is at once simple and decisive. Paul describes as 'dogs'—as excluded from the fellowship of the people of God—those who put a plus-sign after Christ in their teaching about salvation. First they add 'works': they are 'the evil-workers', a phrase which rather means 'evil advocates of (the necessity of) works'. Next they add ceremonial: they are, 'those who mutilate the flesh'. He will not give them the name they would have chosen, 'the circumcision', for he sees that in their obsessive insistence upon this rite they have glorified the mere act, the mere ritual performance as such. Therefore he again perpetrates a deliberate and deserved rudeness, they are 'the mutilators'. These are the men who appear in Acts 15. In verse 1 their doctrine is that 'unless you are circumcised according to the custom of Moses, you cannot be saved'; and verse 5 adds another requirement, namely, 'to charge them to keep the law of Moses'. Thus salvation, while it includes the requirement of belief in Christ, equally needs personal works of righteousness, and the acceptance of a religious ceremony. Thus Christ is not all their boasting; the church and its ceremonies takes a quota; the self and its efforts bears a part. Their 'glory song' should really be, 'Glory be to Christ, and to the church, and to me.' But the song of the redeemed is, 'Glory be to the Father, and to the Son, and to the Holy Ghost.'

'Beware', says Paul. Danger lies this way! Be jealous of the sole and exclusive glory of the Lord; admit no rival; allow no partner! Joy ceases to be joy when it ceases to be '*in the Lord*'.

17 PROFIT AND LOSS

THE WORDS 'NO' AND 'NOT' are perfectly respectable English usage, and in the interest of making the truth clear they have a vital role to fill, for the truth can only be fully safeguarded when its great positive statements are sharpened and clarified by equally great negatives. Paul knew the value of this, and in consequence, when he was led on from his command to 'rejoice in the Lord' to show the Philippians that they could obey it only by holding and practising that religion which was proper to their status as God's covenant people, he not only *affirmed* the work of the Holy Spirit and the centrality of the Lord Jesus, but (in equal and parallel terms) he *denied* the allowability of placing faith in the flesh. His doctrine of salvation required the denial of any and every form of 'do-it-yourself' merit before God.

Gardeners sometimes talk of 'treading in' the roots of a plant in order to ensure proper growth and stability. Paul, who wishes to see the fruit of 'joy in the Lord', and who has told of the root from which it springs, now proceeds to this task of 'treading in'. As we follow him, we will find that it is his purpose to display the uniqueness, and exclusive dignity, and complete satisfactoriness of the Lord Jesus Christ as the basis and the objective of joyful Christian living. But, in his teaching method, before this root can be firmed down, there is the sucker of an alien plant to be eradicated. The positive and the negative aspects must both receive further attention, and first the rank growth must be cleared by the sharp knife of denial.

What does Paul mean by 'the flesh'? It is something in which the Christian is to have 'no confidence'. It is something in which Paul thinks that he himself might have confidence were such confidence allowable. It is something in which men think they may repose confidence. But what is it? It is a description of anyone who is lacking a personal relationship with the Lord Jesus Christ. It must be a common enough business experience to face and carry through the adoption of a whole new method of book-keeping and accounting, and one can imagine a business man recalling (whether with gladness or regret!) 'the year we introduced the new system'. Paul dares to look on Christ in precisely this way in these verses. He looks back to the time—rather, in the light of Acts 9, we should say the day, even the hour and minute—when his whole system of personal spiritual accountancy broke down, and all the accumulated 'profit' of the years slumped to rock bottom and to his astonished gaze there was presented the Christ, whom he had hitherto despised and rejected, as a completely adequate 'credit' which would cover all his needs. 'Whatever gain I had, I counted as loss for the sake of Christ' (verse 7).

We cannot but notice and underline the personal nature of this transaction; its sheer individuality. When Christ met Paul no other stood with them (Acts 9: 5,6; 22: 9; 26: 13 f.). Paul does not dwell in Philippians upon the suddenness of his conversion, but he could hardly make it more personal. Christ became his very own, as real as a cash transaction! This stress upon the glorious individualism of New Testament Christianity is vital to 'joy in the Lord'. We cannot believe that Paul introduced the note of personal testimony in Philippians 3: 4 merely in an illustrative way, and it was certainly not for self-advertisement. It is rather for this reason, that if the 'we' of verse 3 is to have meaning (that is to say if 'we'—the Christian church—are truly to worship by the Spirit of God, glory in Christ Jesus, reject fleshly confidence) it can happen only when 'you' and 'he' and 'she' and 'I' find and possess and treasure Christ for our very own selves.

Now prior to such a possession of Christ, all is 'flesh'. Paul, as described in verses 4–6, is a man describing himself as 'flesh', for he has not yet come into personal possession of Jesus. In other words 'flesh' describes our state from birth until God is pleased to bring us to the new birth (*cf.* Jn. 3: 3–7), or, though this is speaking more loosely, between birth and conversion.

But, if we are to follow Paul's teaching, we must become more specific, for 'flesh', as he uses it here, describes a man who has reached the very pinnacle of moral and religious development. Present-day usage would confine 'flesh' to a description of the rather grosser aspects of immorality; we learn what is our true state before God, and how incredibly marvellous is our Saviour, only when we dismiss this popular conception from our minds, and accept that it is not man at his worst but man at his best who is 'flesh' and therefore not yet acceptable to God.

We see first Paul's natural advantages (verse 5). He had the *ecclesiastical* advantage of full possession of covenant privileges from infancy, having been 'circumcised on the eighth day'. And if we ask 'what is the profit of circumcision?', we can only hear Paul's own answer, 'Much in every way. To begin with, the Jews are entrusted with the oracles of God' (Rom. 3: 2), or again, 'to them belong the sonship, the glory, the covenants, the giving of the law, the worship, and the promises' (Rom. 9: 4). Paul was born to all this, and introduced to his inheritance on the eighth day of life. In addition he claimed the *national* advantage of pure Israelite descent. The descendants of Abraham included the impure line of Ishmael. Isaac was father also to Esau. But Israel was the transformed Jacob from whom sprang the twelve tribes of God's people. Paul's *ancestral* advantage is mentioned next, 'the tribe of Benjamin'. While he was not of Judah, the royal tribe, he was of that tribe which gave the first king to Israel and which later, alone of the other eleven tribes, remained loyal to David and his successors. Finally among his natural advantages he mentions the *parental* benefit, 'a Hebrew born of Hebrews'. He was the child of godly, convinced, zealously religious parents, with all the advantages that brought (*cf.* Lk. 1: 6,15).

Add now to this list of natural advantages the personal acquisitions which Paul claims to have made (verses 5b,6). He speaks of an attitude, an activity, and an achievement. Towards the law of God he adopted the most respectful and submissive attitude possible. He was a Pharisee, 'the strictest party of our religion' (Acts 26:5). His overriding concern was to live in conformity to what he believed were God's regulations for every smallest detail of daily life. So firm was his belief that this alone was the way and will of God that he was zealously active in opposition to every apparent challenge to the dignity of his religion, even to that extent which later so pained him (1 Tim. 1: 13), being 'a persecutor of the church'. But he achieved his goal for he saw himself 'as to righteousness under the law blameless'. And there is no point in our saying, 'Ah, but it was only a legalistic and limited attainment in righteousness.' This is undoubtedly true, but what an attainment it was! Again, there is little point in saying that Paul was assessing his achievement through unregenerate eyes and that his standards were not high enough. This again is true, but what standards they were! A Bostonian who visited Stratford-on-Avon and saw *Hamlet* performed was so enthused as to comment: 'That William Shakespeare was sure some guy! I guess there aren't above twenty men in Boston who could have written that!' But limited as were both Paul's standards and his appraisal at that moment, is it not true to say that we have not met even twenty about whom such a claim could be made? Nor even one? Not even ourselves!

'Flesh' defines the whole life of any and every man, woman, and child who is without living, personal acquaintance with Jesus Christ. It suits those who have sunk lowest in sin, and those who have risen highest in moral, religious, and spiritual rank. Of all alike, the highest as well as the lowest, Jesus Himself said, 'That which is born of the flesh is flesh. . . . Do not marvel that I said to you, "You must be born anew" ' (Jn. 3: 6,7). Let us, however, follow Paul further as, having described what 'flesh' means, he turns to estimate its worth. Remember that his theme here is 'confidence', that is to say, What is it that can make a man confident in the presence of God? Undoubtedly his moral attainments were a great tribute to human endeavour; equally they were a superb influence and contribution to human social well-being: but of what worth were they in giving him confidence before God? Did they fit him for that test? They did not. Man at his most privileged, his most moral, his most religious, his most zealous and devoted, is yet not thereby made fit and acceptable to God. Paul had no recourse but to add up his advantages and achievements one by one and admit that the total was zero! 'Whatever *gain* I had, I counted as *loss* for the sake of Christ' (verse 7). The word 'gain' is plural in the Greek, 'gains'. That is to say, Paul has taken his advantages on the credit side item by item, forgetting nothing, omitting nothing, excluding nothing. All that could be put to his good account is there, his 'gains' each and every one. But when the accountant's eye travels carefully down the list, and the sum total is reckoned, and the line is drawn beneath the completed sum, the answer is an uncompromising singular word, 'loss'. After all has been said, there is nothing and less than nothing for his efforts, and, for certain, no ground of confidence in the sight of God.

But now in the place of 'loss' there stands 'Christ'. How does a person come into possession of Christ who alone is the ground of confidence whereon we can stand before God? It is verse 9 which gives the answer, and presently we will trespass momentarily beyond the bounds of this present study to see it, but first the positive answer must once more be brought into focus by the negatives which arise so clearly from the verses under review. We learn, then, that Christ does not become ours by effort but by rejection of effort. No-one had ever striven for righteousness as did Paul and yet he does not see Christ as the prize standing just above the top rung of the ladder of self-advancement. He cannot have Christ until he has totted up all his works of righteousness and admitted the answer to be 'loss'. 'Not the labours of my hands can fulfil Thy law's demands. . . . Foul (in spite of all my efforts), I to the fountain fly.' Likewise, Christ is not gained by merit but by the repudiation of merit. Were there such a thing as a 'treasury of merit' from which one's personal inadequacies could be met by the superabounding merits of others, Paul would surely have been a beneficiary out of that glorious catalogue of national, ancestral and parental advantages which were his. But before he can call Christ his own these too must be admitted to be 'loss'. Again, Christ is not gained by ecclesiastical ceremony. His circumcision will not save him, although it was a rite commanded by God (Gn. 17), any more than baptism could save Simon the sorcerer (Acts 8: 13,21–23) though that too was of divine origin. Even sacred rites and ceremonies must become items in an addition sum to which the answer is 'loss' if Christ is to be ours.

And if we cannot have Christ we have no other hope. Paul, rejecting as useless all his inherited and acquired virtues, has nothing to put in their place but Christ. These 'I counted as loss *for the sake of Christ*'. He is the only replacement; He is altogether enough; He is Paul's and ours 'through faith' (verse 9). The great missionary John G. Paton, labouring to find a local word which would translate 'faith' and failing to find one, was interrupted by one of his native converts in great trouble and needing help. 'Please, may I come and lean heavily upon you?' he said. Faith is leaning heavily upon Christ, not labour but cessation of labour, not doing but ceasing to do; simply leaning the whole weight of our needs upon Him, and finding in Him acceptance before the presence of God, and a righteousness which could never be ours by our own works.

So Paul came to the end of all his costly striving after acceptance before God through the simplicity of believing in Christ. But at the moment of writing, that experience was long past. It belonged to a far-off day on the road to Damascus. Has Paul no fresh testimony to offer? We notice that present tenses appear in verse 8. Verse 7 records that 'I counted'; verse 8 affirms that 'I count'. It is really here, in fact, that Paul turns to explain what it means to 'glory in Christ Jesus'. He has by now cleared every other potential subject of glory out of the way. All personal merit, all acquired virtue, all efforts after righteousness, all that would be to the glory of man is gone. Christ stands alone on the stage, the *exclusive* (*i.e.* that which excludes all others) object of praise.

We are immediately struck by the fact that the years between the 'counted' of verse 7 and the 'count' of verse 8 have been, for Paul, years of progress. The verses seem to be framed in terms of a deliberate contrast: 'whatever'—*i.e.* a more or less stated number of things—has become 'everything'; 'loss', the estimate then placed upon self-righteousness, is now 'refuse', expressive of positive worthlessness; the bare mention of 'Christ' has been filled out over years of experience of Him so that it is now 'the surpassing worth of knowing Christ Jesus my Lord'. Glorying in Christ Jesus is not a static thing. There will be no joy in the Lord apart from progress in the Lord.

There are four aspects in which Paul notes progress or increase in the years he has known the Lord Jesus. First, there has been a growth of *knowledge* of the Lord. How little he really knew about Jesus that day on the road to Damascus! As, indeed, how little any of us knew about Him at the moment of our conversion! But conversion is not experienced through greatness of knowledge but through simplicity of faith, and the soul passes from darkness to light, and from the power of Satan to God (Col. 1: 13). In honesty, therefore, when Paul gives a testimony of that far-off day he does not pretend something which was not true. 'Christ' is a sufficient summary word. But now there is the 'surpassing worth of knowing Christ Jesus my Lord'. The fullness and wealth of apostolic truth gathered by revelation over the years is in that phrase, as well as the apostle's own intense satisfaction in it and in the Lord. And now he cannot be content with the monosyllabic title. The full glory of the Saviour must be expressed, 'Christ Jesus . . . Lord', and along with it that conviction of personal possession of Christ which has not diminished with the passage of time, nor lost its savour, 'my Lord'.

He has progressed in knowledge, and glories all the more in Christ Jesus because he knows Him more. But greater knowledge has brought another form of increase with it: *consecration*. At his first experience he reckoned as loss everything which he could otherwise have considered as part of his credit balance: 'whatever' (verse 7). Now nothing is held back. For 'the surpassing worth of knowing Christ Jesus my Lord', he says, 'I count *everything* as loss.' How does a Christian achieve total consecration? Progressively, through deeper and deeper knowledge of Christ, for the more He is known the more glorious He is seen to be and the more gladly all is given to and for Him.

But a darker thread was also woven into the progress of the years. They brought an increase of *suffering*, 'for his sake I have suffered the loss of all things'. Paul's consecrated experience was not wholly voluntary. Sometimes he was forced to give up things for Christ; sometimes they were stripped off him by the hands of others. He lost the skin off his back through a Philippian flogging (Acts 16: 22 f.). He lost his liberty in a Caesarean and then a Roman prison; yes, and so much else besides (2 Cor. 11: 23–28). What he told others, he experienced himself, 'through many tribulations we must enter the kingdom of God' (Acts

14: 22), for 'the heirs of salvation, I know from His word, through much tribulation must follow their Lord' (*cf.* Jn. 15: 18–20; 2 Tim. 3: 10–12). In other words there will never be any true glorying in Christ Jesus that is not at some time and in some way a *tested* glorying. Job was not the only one to suffer this testing, and never will be until we are all safely with the Lord (Jb. 1: 9–11; 2: 3–5,10). The point is that glorying in Christ Jesus is not a Christian pastime nor a summer sport but a whole-time occupation and the darker the day the greater the glory to Him when He finds us still rejoicing in the Lord.

Paul's up-to-date testimony brings us one final word. For him the last 'say' does not rest with suffering but with *satisfaction.* He looks candidly at 'everything'; he faces the suffering which has taken it all away; and then he makes his assessment. I 'count them as refuse, in order that I may gain Christ'. Who would want to spend his life on a refuse heap? Far from regretting that they are gone or hankering to have them back, Paul no more wants them around than he wants a bad smell, if this is the appointed road to more and more of Christ. It is Christ, not 'things', who satisfies, and the two words 'gain Christ' would make a fitting motto on the apostle's coat of arms. They cannot be understood to mean that Christ is still eluding him. He has possessed Christ, as verse 7 teaches, since that first great meeting, but how hungry he is for more! To possess Christ, that is the portion of those who are saved and it cannot be taken from them; to be consumed by the ambition to 'gain Christ', that is the driving force in those who are being sanctified. The same Christ who was the only hope for salvation when ceremonies, privileges, religion, and works of righteousness produced nothing but loss, remains to the end the only satisfaction for the Christian. Here is the out-working of the initial command (verse 1) to 'make the Lord your joy'. May we be like Paul in counting Christ alone to be our wealth, and in our determination to see and to evaluate all else in the light of His sole and exclusive satisfactoriness!

18 SATISFIED

'GOD CAN SURELY ASK NOTHING MORE from us than our best.' Over and over again people make this the basis of their hope of eternal salvation—notwithstanding the fact that their hearts, if candidly consulted, would testify that not just once, nor even just a few times, but every single day of their lives they have failed to achieve what they recognize as 'best'. Disregard this universal falling short of even our own highest ideals, however, and consider that Paul achieved his 'best', for 'as righteousness under the law' he was 'blameless'. Yet he gladly exchanged it all for Christ (verse 7) and the passing years made him more and more satisfied with the transaction (verse 8). In dealing with these verses we have already noted that even the highest moral and religious achievements of man without Christ can give no confidence in the presence of God. It was necessary to say this in order to see clearly what Paul was teaching in verses 4–8, but his real assertion of the inadequacy of the 'flesh' comes now in verses 9–12. The setting is much the same: joy in the Lord (verse 1) is rooted in the practice of that true religion which is proper to God's covenant people (verse 3); the centre of that religion is utter and complete satisfaction in Christ. As he now begins to elaborate this satisfaction Paul also reveals the hopeless inadequacy of anything or anyone else to meet the need.

1 SATISFIED TO BE 'FOUND IN HIM' (*verse 9a*)

Paul has just envisaged Christ as a partly possessed wealth which it is his ambition, as time passes, to appropriate more and more completely, 'that I may gain Christ' (verse 8). But now, in order to show more adequately how satisfied he is with Christ, he changes the picture and displays Him as a dwelling-place so attractive, so completely captivating, that he cannot bear ever to be away from home, 'and be found in him'. It may help us to 'feel' Paul's meaning more sharply if we glance back at a similar phrase in 2: 8, 'being found in human form'. What does this mean but that to every chance observer coming upon Him in any place and at any time of day or night the Lord Jesus presented a human appearance and would be judged to be a man? Bishop Moule (*CB*) is thus able to explain Paul's longing to be 'found' in Christ as meaning that 'at any moment of scrutiny or test; alike in life, death, and before the judgment seat' this will be his situation. Or again, we might put it this way. A friend going on a journey and being uncertain of his future whereabouts might say, 'But you can always address a letter to me at . . .' Likewise Paul! He may be in Rome, Caesarea, Jerusalem, Philippi; he may be in want or wealth; he may be sick, healthy, worried, free of care—but he will always be 'in him'. Thus his satisfaction in Christ is the deepest of all; there is nothing to compare with it.

II SATISFIED TO BE BLESSED BY HIM (*verse 9b*)

In this 'permanent address' of his, 'in Christ', there was one especial treasure which shed its lustre over the entire house: *righteousness*. When he is in Christ Paul can describe himself as 'not having a righteousness of my own, based on law, but that which is through faith in Christ, the righteousness from God that depends on faith'. The notion of righteousness dominates this description of the man 'in Christ'. There is a righteousness which will not satisfy ('not . . . a righteousness of my own'); there is a righteousness which meets the need ('the righteousness from God') which, as regards the way in which it may be acquired, is the righteousness 'which is through faith in Christ'.

The simplest definition of 'righteousness' will suffice for our understanding of what Paul is saying. It means 'in the right'. And Paul has particularly in mind what is involved if a man is to be 'in the right' before God. How is it possible for him to be sure that when God examines him the verdict will be 'Paul is in the right', 'Paul is all that I require him to be', 'Paul is righteous'?

a. The righteousness which he abandons

Being 'found in him', Paul has no wish for 'a righteousness of my own, based on law'. There are two things taught here: how such a righteousness is achieved, and what its character is. As to its achievement, it is 'of my own'; it is a 'do-it-yourself' righteousness; it has arisen through self-effort or personal good works. These good works have been patterned on a legal code, and hence it is a righteousness 'based on law'. Paul had once been able to boast of such a righteousness when it was his claim that he was 'as to the law a Pharisee . . . as to righteousness under the law blameless'. His own intense, demanding, sacrificial labours had produced conformity to a legal code of behaviour.

Of what worth was this conformist righteousness? Just that and nothing more, a 'certificate of good behaviour'! It was a righteousness 'based on law', literally 'out from the law', such a righteousness as proceeds from conforming to a standard. Now, such a righteousness is without security. It can furnish no confidence concerning God's judgment of us, and that for two reasons: first, because, even if we ever did attain such an unbroken record, we have still to maintain it until the judgment day, and one slip is enough to make the law pronounce an adverse verdict whereby our 'righteousness' evaporates into nothing. But, more important, secondly, such a righteousness is self-conferred. We have weighed our own merits, examined our own right to the verdict. We have been both defendant and judge. We could never be certain that our verdict would command God's respect, nor that our prejudiced and partial self-knowledge was as penetrating as the eyes of His holy scrutiny. In particular we might pass ourselves 'A.1' by overlooking our inner defections from the path of obedience—just as Paul found himself beaten by the law when he faced its condemnation of the covetous heart (Rom. 7: 7). A certificate of good behaviour which we have awarded to ourselves is not enough to give us confidence as we face the judgment of God.

b. The righteousness which he desires

There is, however, the possibility of a certificate of righteousness which God awards, and in this case we can indeed be confident. For if God pronounces us 'right' with Him, then we are indeed secure for ever. This is what Christ means to Paul, and it is this which sheds lustre on his satisfaction at being 'found in him'. He tells us of its origin, the condition on which it is offered, and the way in which it is personally appropriated.

As to its origin, it is 'the righteousness *from God*', and here again the word means 'out from'. This righteousness proceeds out from God; it is His award. The importance of this cannot be overstressed. There can be no salvation apart from God being satisfied. Christ might die (may we say it reverently) a thousand deaths; sin might be cleansed away a thousand times; but if God is not satisfied with what is done then it is all a waste of time, effort, and suffering. If God will not have us back then every effort to bring us back is misconceived and pointless. But here is a salvation for sinners which has as its first principle that God is satisfied with it. It is a righteousness which 'proceeds *out from God*'. Therefore it is certain from the outset.

Secondly, it is offered on condition of *faith,* 'the righteousness from God that depends on *faith*'. Here, then, is the simplicity and freeness of this salvation. Gone are the exertions of law-keeping, gone the disciplines and asceticisms of legalism, gone the anxiety lest having done everything we have yet not done enough. The goal is reached not by the stairs but by the lift. 'Faith' is the abandonment of works and efforts, and the promised righteousness of God is pledged to those who will cease trying to save themselves.

But this is not any old faith! There is a 'faith' (so-called) which is nothing more or less than credulity. Faith is valuable only when it is reposed in a trustworthy object. Of supreme value, then, is the righteousness which is ours 'through faith in Christ'. How utterly and completely marvellous! We rely upon the very Son of God Himself to bring us home acceptably to God. The Son of God is the Mediator of the righteousness of God to those who place their faith in Him.

III SATISFIED TO BE MADE LIKE HIM (*verse 10*)

So free is this salvation, and so completely independent of any efforts or merits of ours, that it is open to the accusation of making a virtue of sin. Paul faced this charge, 'Why not do evil that good may come?—as some people slanderously charge us with saying' (Rom. 3: 8). For surely, if while we were sinners God showed this astounding mercy to us, ought we not to go on sinning and thus provoke even more astounding mercy? If, apart from our works and merits, God has so signally blessed us with His gift of righteousness, ought we not to continue without works and merits and thus secure additional benefits? Let us note that the very fact that it is open to this charge is proof that Paul preached a completely free salvation, for if he had given any slightest suggestion that we are in the smallest part saved by our own efforts his slanderers could not have thus reported his sermons. Salvation is indeed as free as that!

But the saved have been given God's gift of 'righteousness', and righteousness carries with it inevitably the meaning of 'right living'. It is because of this that Paul proceeds from verse 9, in which he has taught 'free salvation', to verse 10, in which he shows the Christian as thus introduced into the sphere of the strictest moral enterprise and endurance. Characteristically, Paul delineates it as becoming like Christ. Surely, if a person is satisfied with Christ for salvation, he cannot rest until he is like the One who satisfies him so.

The topic of Christlikeness is introduced in a way which would surprise us were we not so used to reading it here, 'that I may know him'. We have largely lost the biblical dimensions of the word 'knowledge' in our customary use of it. We confine it almost entirely to 'the contents of the brain'. The Bible would not resist this meaning, but neither would it accept it as a complete definition. First, it would add a practical dimension. Nothing is truly known unless it is being practised in daily life, or in some way (according to its nature) allowed to control the conduct of the person concerned—'to depart from evil is understanding' (Jb. 28: 28). Secondly, in knowledge between persons, to 'know' is to enter into the deepest personal intimacy and contact. Thus the Bible does not say that 'Adam knew Eve' (Gn. 4: 1) because it is too shy to speak openly about sexual matters, but because this is what knowledge between persons is—deep, intimate union. Consequently, having been saved wholly and solely by Christ, Paul wants to enter into the deepest possible union with Him. He wants 'to know him'.

What does this involve? The career of Christ, as depicted in 2: 5–11, was one of descent into death leading through into the glory of the resurrection. To be made like Christ, to enter into intimate union with Him, to know Him, necessarily involves the same experiences, 'becoming like him in his death, that if possible I may attain the resurrection from the dead'. How surprised we often are when (as we say) life brings its trials to us! But what did we expect? Do we want to be made like Christ or not? Christlikeness must lead us to Calvary. We must be ready for —and we cannot hope to avoid—the downward path of the Crucified. It was true of Paul: down to the dungeon and thence to the executioner's block, and 'all who desire to live a godly life in Christ Jesus will be persecuted' (2 Tim. 3: 12). The servant must be made like his Lord (Jn. 15: 20). We must not 'be surprised at the fiery ordeal . . . as though something strange were happening. . . . But rejoice in so far as you share Christ's sufferings' (1 Pet. 4: 12 f.). This is the way the Lord Jesus went, and it is the way of Christlikeness for us.

But in dwelling on 'becoming like him in his death' we have taken the verse out of order and we must now retrace our steps and see what encouragements Paul uses as brackets round this reality of the cross in the experience of the Christian. First let us ask why he speaks of the resurrection of Christ before he has mentioned His death? Surely he has reversed the events of our Lord's experience? Indeed he has, but with a deliberate purpose. For Christ, death preceded resurrection, but for the Christian who sets out to follow his Lord along this path the power of the risen Christ is the first fact of his experience. Thus, as we walk the path of Christlikeness in an apostolic determination to 'be made like Him', even to the extent of sharing His sufferings, His risen power is made available to strengthen, keep and lead us through.

More than that, however, is available. For again, before he spoke of 'becoming like him in his death' Paul referred to 'sharing', or 'fellowship' in, His sufferings. Why does he thus make a double reference to the cross of Christ? It is for this reason, that he wants us to see that in desiring to follow Him as faithful cross-bearers we are not left alone; He keeps fellowship with us; we are not copying a dead Model but walking in fellowship with a living Saviour.

These emphases on power and companionship are our encouragements on the way, but there is also the encouragement of the goal, '. . . the resurrection from the dead' (verse 11). We could be misled by 'if possible', which seems to suggest that, after all, Paul was not sure of final salvation. If the verse meant this, it would not only be discordant with verse 9, but would flatly contradict 1: 23, and many other passages (*e.g.* 2 Cor. 5: 1; Rom. 8: 38 f.) in Paul's writings. Yet this verse does express uncertainty, but uncertainty of the way, not of the goal. The resurrection is certain; the intervening events are uncertain. We neither know how many days we have left on earth nor what those days will contain, but we do know that be they many or few, smooth or rough, at the end of them there is the glory, 'the resurrection from the dead'. Paul, therefore, encourages himself and us along the path of Christlikeness by sharing openly his determination, as though he said, 'so that by whatever route God in His providence shall ordain—and what it will be I do not know—empowered by Christ and accompanied by Christ I will follow Him, bearing my cross, descending with Him into death, and then for all eternity, still with Him, enjoying the glory of the resurrection'.

IV SATISFIED TO SATISFY HIM (*verse 12*)

We come at the end of our study to a 'stock-taking' verse. Paul has expressed his readiness to 'go all the way' with Christ, so complete is his satisfaction in Him. Now he pauses to assess the past ('not that I have already obtained'), the present ('I press on'), and the future ('to make it my own', *cf.* RV).

Three great truths are stated here. First, *the new perceptions of the converted man.* We observed above that if we presume to be both defendant and judge in our own trials then we may not in fact arrive at a correct estimate of ourselves. We now see that that is indeed the case. Once upon a time Paul thought that he had 'arrived', for he judged himself 'as to righteousness under the law blameless' (verse 6). But now hear his estimate, 'Not that I have already obtained this or am already perfect.' Sinless perfection is not the experience even of an apostle this side of glory! He sees himself with new eyes, for he has been illumined with spiritual understanding. He has not 'arrived', he is not perfect, much land remains to be occupied. He sees it as his personal responsibility to 'press on', and this also is one of the new perceptions of the converted man. The same Paul who in respect of salvation counselled cessation of effort (verse 9), in respect of sanctification says 'I press on'. The word is vigorous: 'I pursue, I persecute.' It is a rigorous, determined, single-minded activity. Paul is out after his prey, as once he 'persecuted' the church (verse 6)!

Secondly, we learn what is *the inner reality of conversion,* 'Christ Jesus has made me his own.' The memory of conversion is sweet: the well remembered reaching out of the personal but empty hand of faith to Jesus. But behind it, making it possible, giving it reality, there was the act of God apprehending the individual. Did Paul choose Christ? Indeed he did, but only because first Christ chose Paul, and in comparison with each other the act of God so surpasses in importance the responsive activity of man that the Lord Jesus Himself said, 'You did not choose me, but I chose you' (Jn. 15: 16). It is this that gives us security and confidence. We are 'in Christ' because of His changeless, inflexible will that it should be so.

Finally, here is *the sole objective of the converted man,* 'to make it my own' (or as RV expresses it 'that for which also I was apprehended by Christ Jesus'). What did He have in mind when He took me? What was His purpose? What end was in view? The purposes are as many as there are individuals in Christ. For each there are the 'good works, which God prepared beforehand, that we should walk in them' (Eph. 2: 10). But for every converted person Paul here holds up the same ideal: whatever Christ's goal and objective is, no pains will be spared to achieve it. The more a person is satisfied with Christ the more he will find his satisfaction in satisfying Him.

19 ON TO MATURITY

A BIRD'S-EYE VIEW OF VERSES 13–21 reveals that they are held together by two repeated ideas. According to verses 15 and 17 Christians are called to model themselves deliberately on the pattern set by Paul, and according to verses 14 and 20 this apostolic pattern of life is to be lived out by keeping our gaze steadfastly upon the future. The 'calls' issued by verses 15 and 17 are not substantially different from each other, but the future on which we are to look is variously expressed by the other two verses. According to verse 14, there is a goal to be *attained,* and according to verse 20 there is a Saviour to be *awaited*. Thus, there are two aspects to the life modelled on the apostolic pattern. On the one hand it is a life of personal commitment, effort, and determination (verses 13,14); on the other hand, it is a life resting upon great certainties, in particular the abiding truths of the cross (verses 18,19) and the coming (verses 20,21) of the Lord Jesus. It is a life, therefore, of consecration and conviction.

Turning now particularly to verses 13–16, it is easy to see that they fall into two sections. We find Paul's example in verses 13,14, as he continues the personal testimony which started in verse 4 and shares with us his determinations for the remainder of his life on earth. Verses 15,16 turn to the task of exhortation. Paul has not spoken of himself out of a spirit of display but to provide a guide to the church and a standard of Christian living to which other Christians may be called. It will help us to place a proper emphasis upon Paul's example if we study these two sections in reverse order.

I PAUL'S EXHORTATION (*verses 15,16*)
He addresses the 'mature' or (RV) 'perfect', calling them to have the same attitude towards life ('thus minded') as he has. What does 'perfect' mean? Sometimes it means 'fully perfect' (*e.g.* Mt. 5: 48) but that cannot be its meaning here for, using virtually the same word in verse 12, Paul disclaims any idea of being already the finished article, and even in this verse itself those who are described as 'perfect' are being exhorted to match the apostle in 'pressing on' to the goal. Bengel suggests that the RV words 'made perfect' (verse 12) and 'perfect' (verse 15) are both drawn from the vocabulary of the athletics track. 'Perfect' means 'fit' or 'in training'; 'made perfect' means 'crowned as victor', 'having attained the prize'. This meaning is born out by the usage in Hebrews 10: 14, 'By a single offering he has perfected (made perfect) for all time those who are (being) sanctified.' Viewed in the light of the finished work of Calvary, Christians are already 'made perfect', crowned and rewarded in Christ (*cf.* Eph. 2: 5,6); but viewed in the light of their own experience they are still 'on the way', still 'being sanctified'. Consequently, Paul is addressing the person who is *fully established* in Christ and who is *zealous to go on to maturity*. What he is setting before us here is a recipe for Christian growth and progress.

Paul believed himself to hold a key place in relation to other Christians. Elsewhere he asserted his authority as an apostle in matters of doctrine (*e.g.* 1 Cor. 2: 10–13; 14: 37; 1 Thes. 2: 13) requiring that what he taught be received as the commandment of God. But here he makes a similar claim regarding his manner of life. The movement of thought is as follows, 'Brethren I want to let you know with what thoughts and resolves I face the future (verses 13,14), *therefore* (verse 15) I am setting a pattern for all established Christians to follow.' He is absolutely certain about this, for when he envisages (verse 15b) that some at Philippi may hold a contrary opinion as to the way of Christian growth, he continues, 'God will reveal that also to you', that is to say, God will lead you round to the same way of thinking as me. This stupendous claim has a twofold bearing on our study of these verses. First, it is part of the New Testament evidence for the uniqueness of the apostolic band. Since the days of Paul and his fellow apostles, just as none have been able to say, 'Am I not an apostle? Have I not seen Jesus our Lord?' (1 Cor. 9: 1), and none have been able to say, 'The gospel which was preached by me . . . came through a revelation of Jesus Christ' (Gal. 1: 12), so none have been able to say, 'Be imitators of me, as I am of Christ' (1 Cor. 11: 1). The apostolic band had the unique and unrepeatable position of church-founders, being organs of revelation, infallible teachers, and divinely given examples to the church. The church today is apostolic, not by its possession of (so-called) apostolic men, but by its adherence to the apostolic doctrine and example taught in the Holy Scriptures.

Secondly, Paul's claim that his manner of life is divinely authorized ('God will reveal that also to you') makes verses 13,14 of immense importance, practically, for the Christian. In all the tangles and ramifications of argument concerning the doctrine of sanctification and the means of sanctification in the life of the Christian here is a certain guide. For what is sanctification but a summary term for 'making progress in the Christian life'? Very well then, here is the apostolic pattern for the progressing Christian, sanctification according to Paul.

However, even though Paul knew himself to possess this exalted authority in the church, the spirit in which he writes to the Philippians in these verses is very far from authoritarian, in the 'bad' sense of that word. Bishop Moule wrote at one point in the margin of his Greek Testament the comment '*apostolus, non papa!*'—'An apostle, not a Pope!' Paul possessed authority. He did not exercise dictatorship. And we may well pause here to note the nature of Paul's leadership in the church. Consider how he says 'Brethren' (verse 13), and 'us' (verse 15). Apostle though he is, yet he is also a believer amongst other believers, needing their fellowship (*cf.* 1: 19) and taking a common stand with them in the pursuit of progress. Notice how he does not say to the disagreeing person, 'If you are otherwise minded, look out! I am the arbiter of such matters.' He says, 'God will reveal it.' Notice, finally, the rule of progress enunciated in verse 16. Each man is to take responsibility for his own walk, and to walk up to the limit of the light given him. Apostolic authority left scope for individual responsibility, and left the individual in charge of his own progress. '*Only*', he says (verse 16), that is to say, 'Understand all that I have told you in the light of *this one thing*: you have already attained some standing in Christ, walk by the rule of what you have already learned. This is your way forward.'

Paul insists on the exercise of private judgment as essential if the individual Christian is to grow in Christ. He would undoubtedly have agreed with the marvellously exact words of Hooker (*Ecclesiastical Polity,* VI. vi. 2) in comparing the Roman and the Protestant attitude towards the individual Christian: 'We labour to instruct men in such sort, that every soul that is wounded with sin may learn the way how to cure itself; they, clean contrary, would make all sores incurable unless a priest have a hand in them.' According to Paul, the one is the way of repression and the other the way of growth, and thus he insists that each Christian makes his own speed, walks as God has taught him, and lives to the full limit of the standard of maturity which he has already attained. In the last analysis the Christian is the individual sheep directly under the shepherding hand of God, 'God will reveal that also to you.'

II PAUL'S EXAMPLE (*verses 13,14*)

We ought to come to these verses, then, with a due sense of their importance. They are Paul's recipe for progress in the Christian life, and that in itself commends and commands them to us. But in his estimation they are also God's scheme, for, he urges, all who seek the mind of God will be led to this same conclusion. Here, then, is the formula for Christian growth.

a. A correct self-estimate

'Brethren, I do not consider that I have made it my own' (verse 13a). Part of Paul's self-estimate here is, of course, the use of the word 'brethren', his recognition of the spiritual equality of all believers, but we have already noticed this point, and will move on to what Paul actually says about himself. The word 'made it my own' derives its meaning from verse 12. It has reference to the will of Christ for Paul (*cf.* RV). In calling Paul to Himself, God had in mind both His common will for all the redeemed, 'that we should be holy and blameless before him in love' (Eph. 1: 4, mg.), and also His particular will for Paul's life and service

(Eph. 2: 10). Paul recognizes that he has not yet attained to all that God purposed for him, nor made it his own. Knowing Christ has brought Paul to a very different self-estimate from that which his Pharisaic up-bringing had inculcated (verse 6), and a more realistic and sobering one at that.

If we were to ask ourselves what is the primary characteristic of a Christian, it is very likely that the majority reply would be 'love', and, of course, there is great biblical ground for this (*cf.* 1: 9), but there is equal if not more ground for saying 'humble-mindedness' or 'a correct lowly estimate of oneself'. This is the first virtue commended in Romans 12: 3 as the mark of the 'presented' or consecrated Christian, 'not to think of himself more highly than he ought to think'. The same injunction opens the practical section of teaching in Ephesians (4: 1) as the mark of the life which is worthy of the Christian calling, 'with all lowliness', where the word really means 'humble-mindedness', a lowly estimate of oneself. Likewise, again, in Philippians 2: 3 it is the mark of 'the worthy life', 'in humility count others better than yourselves'. We do well to recall that the Lord Jesus put first in the Sermon on the Mount the blessedness of the man who is 'poor in spirit', aware of his own wretchedness, the very reverse of proud self-sufficiency. Here is the spring of progress.

b. A single-minded zeal

There is an impressive *activity* about the progressing Christian. This is not a new feature introduced here for the first time into Paul's teaching to the Philippians. We have only to recall the 'stand firm' of 1: 27, the 'work' of 2: 12, the 'run' and 'labour' of 2: 16, the bond-service of 2: 22, or the 'nearly died' of 2: 30 to realize that there is no room for idleness in the Christian, and here, when Paul is speaking primarily of his own personal growth as a Christian, his 'sanctification', he shows himself as one shouldering the responsibility and getting on with the job. Sanctification leaves no room for spiritual relaxation.

Equally impressive is the emphasis upon *concentration*. If we treat the Greek literally we find, '*One thing!* Forgetting the things which are behind . . . I press on. . . .' Needless to say we are not to imagine Paul forgetting God's past mercies, for he has been dwelling most forcibly upon them since verse 7! Nor are we to imagine that he forgets past lessons, for these too have occupied him in this very chapter (verses 2–6). What then does he mean by this forgetting of the past? There is a dwelling upon the past which clogs the wheels of present endeavour and future progress. With all tenderness we might say that sometimes a bereavement makes even a convinced believer 'live in the past', or again a notable collapse from the standards of Christ might cause a believer to despair of ever rising to live for Him again—and many other suchlike things. We may recall for our learning how vigorously the angel acted in Zechariah 2: 1–4 to forbid the man who proposed to measure the dimensions of the ruins of Jerusalem. The same spirit is still with us, the spirit which rules the future by the achievements of the past. The progressing Christian must cultivate the concentrated gaze of a person living in the future.

This requires *determination*: 'straining forward . . . I press on'. It seems beyond question that Paul is again drawing his picture from the athletics meeting. Here is the runner 'extended' in every fibre of his being, 'The eye outstrips and draws on the hand, and the hand the foot' (Bengel). The whole being is at a stretch to cross the line. Then, changing the metaphor, Paul says, 'I press on', and again it really means, 'I pursue, I persecute'. No obsessive hatred ever dogged the heels of its adversary with more tenacity than the apostle held on to the target of Christian perfection. And yet how often we hear preachers telling Christian congregations that the appointed way of sanctification is to 'let go and let God'! There was not much 'letting go' about Paul, but a clear example that the sanctifying grace of God is appropriated by the obedient and unrelenting activity of the regenerate man.

c. An absorbing desire

What is it that holds the apostle's gaze so that he leaves the past and is wholly occupied with the future? It is 'the goal . . . the prize . . .' In one other place Paul uses this word to refer to the prize. Writing to the Corinthians, familiar as they were with the Corinthian Games, he reminded them that 'in a race all the runners compete, but only one receives the prize. So run that you may obtain it' (1 Cor. 9: 24). Note the individual responsibility: each man out to get the prize for himself! Paul does not pause to say what the prize is, but we know from other scriptures what he would have in mind. There is the Master's 'well done' (*cf.* Lk. 19: 17); there is 'the crown of righteousness, which the Lord, the righteous judge, will award to me on that Day, and not only to me but also to all who have loved his appearing' (2 Tim. 4: 8); there is the 'unfading crown of glory' given by the chief Shepherd (1 Pet. 5: 4); there is such a thing as not being ashamed before Him at His coming (1 Jn. 2: 28). This is the prize which awaits the apostle at 'the goal', the tape marking the end of the course.

d. A sure foundation

All this activity is not 'whistling in the dark'; it is not the panic of a man trying by every means to make certain of something towards which he feels basically insecure. In this tremendously active doctrine of sanctification which Paul is preaching by his practice here, he is not abandoning justification by faith; he is not deserting the freeness of salvation. It is in fact (exactly as we saw in relation to 2: 12,13) because both salvation and sanctification have been perfectly and fully accomplished for us by Christ (*cf.* Heb. 10: 10–14) that we are able to appropriate the one by the response of faith apart from works, and the other by the response of faithful obedience in works.

Paul ends his delineation of his example on this note of security and certainty. The prize towards which he is drawn in disciplined and concentrated activity is described as belonging to ('of') 'the upward call (or 'high calling') of God in Christ Jesus'. A study of the idea of 'calling' in the Epistles of Paul will reveal that its meaning is not 'invitation' into gospel privileges but 'the actual prevailing power of God over the wills of His people' (Moule, *PS*). It is not God's invitation to be saved; it is God's determination to save. The prize is part of, and is guaranteed by, God's saving purposes at work in Paul, and in all His called children (*cf.* Rom. 8: 29–39). It is for this reason that, in the other passage where he mentions 'prize', Paul depicts himself fighting '*not as aimlessly*' or '*uncertainly*' (1 Cor. 9: 26). His final salvation, with all the glories of its rewards, was secured for him by and with God's calling of him in Christ.

Sovereign Lord and gracious Master,
Thou didst freely choose thine own;
Thou hast called with holy calling;
Thou wilt save and keep from falling;
Thine the glory, thine alone.
Yet thine hand shall crown in heaven
All the grace thy love hath given,
Just though undeserved reward,
From our glorious, gracious Lord.

F. R. HAVERGAL

20 ENEMIES OF THE CROSS

THERE IS ONLY ONE FORM OF APOSTOLIC SUCCESSION worth bothering about. It is that which Paul commands here when he says, 'Join in imitating me . . . have an example in us.' He is, of course, reiterating verse 15 and therefore calling us again to copy that apostolic life which is described in verses 8–14. But at the same time, both in the setting of this repeated command, and in the incidentals of its expression, he adds three elements of fundamental importance to his outline of apostolic living. If we are to imitate him, then we must be like him not only in our growing delight in Christ (verse 8), our reliance on Him alone for salvation (verse 9), our determination to be like Him and to do His will (verses 10–12), and our single-minded, active pursuit of the prize (verses 13,14). We must also esteem truth as he did, marry truth to love, and balance individualism with pastoral care.

First, we must observe the fundamental place occupied by the truth in apostolic living. We note that when Paul orders us to follow his example he adds an explanation: 'For (verse 18) . . .' This is therefore a different call to Christians from that issued in verse 15. In that verse he spoke broadly as follows: 'My way of life is the pattern for you all; if you do not see it like this now, wait upon God and He will reveal to you that it is so.' In other words, the apostolic way of life is in accord with the will of God. But in verses 17–20 he speaks rather differently, and we might sum up his thought thus: 'Imitate me because only by doing so will you live the life that accords with the truth about the cross (verse 18) and the coming (verse 20) of the Lord Jesus Christ.' In other words, when the *truth*—and especially the truth about the cross and the return—is properly grasped, this way of life naturally follows. We can see exactly the same relationship of things in Paul's last testament to Timothy. Leaving that rather nervous young man in a most frightening situation (2 Tim. 3:1–9), his reassurance to him opens with the words, 'Now you have observed my teaching, my conduct . . .': first the truth and then the way of life that arises from the truth. Likewise, the Lord Jesus Himself underlined the same relationship when He not only said 'the Son makes you free' but also 'the truth will make you free' (Jn. 8: 36,32). Or again, writing to Titus, Paul throughout emphasized that 'sound doctrine' and 'good works' cannot be separated. His accusation against some is that 'they profess to *know* God; but they deny him by their *deeds*' (Tit. 1: 16). On the contrary, his desire for the Christians is that 'they may *adorn the doctrine* of God our saviour' (Tit. 2: 10).

Thus instruction, knowledge, grasp of the truth, knowing the answers (1 Pet. 3: 15) are not Christian options, or the duty of the few. They are fundamental to following in the succession of the apostles, and, indeed, it is for this reason that God has given us the Holy Scriptures. But there is a second element in the apostolic example which we must hasten to add to this one. The truth must be married to love. Paul was a great weeper. He shed great tears in his yearning for the Ephesians (Acts 20: 19,31); he cried over the Corinthians when he had to issue an apostolic rebuke (2 Cor. 2: 4); and here again we find him full of tears, with the difference that here he *weeps* for those about whom he must *warn*. We have already heard some of Paul's denunciatory warnings, 'Look out for . . . dogs . . . evil-workers . . .' (verse 2). How easy it would be to import into our reading of these words the harshness which we would feel towards people whom we judged worthy of such names! But even as Paul denounces, or exposes as a solemn warning, he weeps for their souls. It is only to our sub-apostolic standards and sub-apostolic experience of Christ that love and clear-headed contradiction are thought to be mutually exclusive. In Paul we see the perfect marriage of truth and love, and this also is part of his example bequeathed to us. He will not leave us until he has shown us how this may come to pass.

We may proceed at once to the third new feature in Paul's example. He has shown himself as the zealous individualist, all out for his own spiritual growth and attainment of the prize. The prize-winner dare not pause to help others over the hurdles! But see here another side of the apostle, when he weeps with care for the souls of men, and when he takes pains to lead the Philippians in the way of Christ. Individual care for one's own spiritual progress is not inconsistent with pastoral responsibility for the souls and welfare of others. The Christian who has no right to expect anything else but that he must bear his own load (Gal. 6: 5) must be ready at all times to bear the other man's burden (Gal. 6: 2). Nevertheless, there is a due priority to be observed, for Paul depicted himself as the zealous runner before he turned to be the zealous pastor (verses 13,14,17,18). It must always be so. 'Take heed *to yourselves* and *to all the flock*' (Acts 20: 28); or again, more personally, 'Take heed *to yourself* and to *your teaching*' (1 Tim. 4: 16). We can never help keep another man's vineyard if we neglect our own, but the apostolic example says to us, 'This you should have done, and not have left the other undone.' Both activities are equally obligatory.

I CONTRAST

Having observed these incidental aspects of Paul's example, we must now turn to the main line of his teaching. He has already outlined his manner of life (verses 8–14) and called for unanimity (verse 15) and imitation (verse 17). Now in order to sharpen our awareness of what it is that he is asking of us he once more engages in some denials. He focuses attention upon the life he requires by setting in contrast the life he rejects. We will better know what to follow by knowing what to avoid.

We do not know, of course, who precisely he is warning us against. Some say that these 'enemies of the cross' are again the 'Judaizers', the 'Christ-plus' men of verse 2. Some say that he is warning against the sin of antinomianism, the sin of those who abuse their liberty in Christ, making it an open licence to every sort of indulgence (*cf.* Rom. 3: 8; 6: 1). Or, equally, he could be warning against the pull of the world, ever the enticing open door to depart from the way of Christ (*cf.* Rom. 12: 2a). In the long run it is of no odds who he is decrying, and it is better not to attach the verses too firmly to any bygone situation, for the threat is still present to the Christian, as we shall see, and the description is perfectly clear even if names are absent.

First, Paul says that 'their end is destruction'. He looks beyond this world to the next and finds no hope at all for them there, nothing but eternal loss. The same fate awaits them as awaits the opposing world (1: 28), and the 'beast' of Revelation 17: 11, a fate subsequently described as 'the lake of fire' (Rev. 19: 20) and 'the second death' (Rev. 20: 14). Bible students differ as to how this is to be understood, and it would take us far off course to enter into details. It is enough to know that their ultimate end is an eternal and irreversible separation from God. But the 'end' for Paul, the goal and outcome of the apostolic life is very far different, 'the prize of the upward call of God in Christ Jesus' (verse 14; *cf.* 1: 23).

Secondly, they worship themselves, 'their god is the belly'. They are entirely satisfied with themselves and recognize no need and no authority outside personal satisfaction. Their appetites dictate their lives. Again, this is not the apostolic way. Paul, who had 'no confidence in the flesh' (verse 3), testified to being far from perfect ('not that I have already obtained this or am already perfect', verse 12), and very far from being content with present attainments ('straining forward . . . I press on . . .', verses 13,14). Thus, again, two ways of life are in contrast.

Thirdly, they find cause to glory in things of which they ought to be ashamed. Their code of behaviour justifies as allowable things which it ought to condemn, but Paul was wholly absorbed in 'glorying in Christ Jesus' (verses 3,7–12) and in putting forth every effort in order to attain what Christ had purposed for his life. The contrast here is between making the self and making the Christ the moral authority for life.

Finally there is a contrast of horizons. They are earth-bound. Their minds are 'set on things'. Their whole attention, their point of view or way of looking at things, their general frame of mind, their customary objects of study—all these are earth-centred and bounded by the horizons of this world. But Paul's eyes are on heaven, and the prize of the heavenly calling (verse 14).

Why does Paul go out of his way to depict this contrasting life? Because he must warn against it. This is no external danger or far-off contingency. He sees his Philippians as faced daily by this contrary example, 'mark those who so live' (verse 17). There are two ways of life constantly inviting the obedience of the Christian, and Paul had nothing else to offer but the constant pulling of the one against the other. There is no recipe for 'peace' (so-called) here. There is no promise of deliverance from the struggle and the tension and the persistent temptation. Like Israel of old, the Christian of today stands between the blessing and the cursing, the way of life and the way of death (*cf.* Dt. 30: 19) and the whole Christian pathway is the battle to choose life. This is the meaning of the stark contrast between the life of the apostle and the life of those whom he calls enemies of the cross. Faithfully and in love to our souls Paul has raised the warning sign.

II DIAGNOSIS

Since we can never escape the pull of temptation till we are safe with Christ it will be well to dwell a little on Paul's diagnosis in order that we may see more precisely the character of those whose end is destruction. As they progress towards this end, there are three points of spiritual degeneration: their 'god is the belly', their 'glory (is) in their shame', and their minds are 'set on earthly things'.

The first point at which they are spiritually degenerating is *their devotion to self-indulgence*. Their appetites and emotions have ceased to be subject to them and have been accorded the place of lordship and worship. They are governed by self-pleasing in bodily matters. Consider that Paul does not elaborate. He does not call them fornicators or alcoholics. There is no particularizing of their pet sensualities. If he did so we might stand aloof from the warning if the particular indulgence did not happen to appeal to us or to be our temptation. The warning is not against this or that, but against the thing itself, pandering to self. In one Christian the temptation may be towards sexual sin, in another towards giving rein to a gossiping tongue, in another towards lying in bed when he should be alone with God in the morning. Paul raises the warning. Here is the downward path and those who walk it are enemies of the cross of Christ. There must have been many mature believers in the church at Rome, for Paul was inspired to write to them his major doctrinal Epistle. But he did not scorn to call them away from revelling and drunkenness, debauchery and licentiousness (13: 13), for the bodily sin is never far beneath the surface even of the most advanced saint and the warning is ever needful.

Paul's second observation as he diagnoses spiritual degeneration is *their reversal of moral standards*. They 'glory in their shame'. In other words they exalt things and practices which they ought to be ashamed of but are not. Clearly this is the next stage downward. First they give themselves to indulgence; next they justify themselves in doing so and say that this is a proper and allowable way of life. Long ago the prophet Isaiah saw the very same thing in the life of his nation. He observed those who 'call evil good and good evil' and he noted two aspects of their reversal of moral standards: they 'put darkness for light and light for darkness' and they 'put bitter for sweet and sweet for bitter' (Is. 5: 20). Light and darkness are objective facts governing all alike. By this illustration he shows how they tried to make their topsy-turvy moral code a law of public behaviour. Bitter and sweet vary from person to person. By this illustration he showed that their public code was rooted in their life of self-pleasing. So it is with those whom Paul describes, but once more he does not particularize. There is no dwelling upon this reversal of morals or that, but upon the thing itself. The warning has been given. Here is the downward path and those who walk it are enemies of the cross of Christ. We are sometimes inclined to think that no day has ever been like ours in attempting to reverse moral standards. This is most unlikely to be true, but what is true is that now, as always, the world is preaching its own standards and very, very often they are not the standards of God's Word. The Christian must remember that he is called not only to believe revealed doctrine but to obey revealed law, and the *book of the law* should not depart from his mouth, but he should meditate in it day and night in order to make *his way*, his public life and conduct, prosperous (Jos. 1 : 8).

In the final diagnosis the root of their trouble is discovered in *their cultivation of an earthly mind*: their 'minds (are) set on earthly things'. At the very centre of their being, where their life finds its direction, where the attitudes and tendencies are fashioned which subsequently influence decisions and govern likes and dislikes—at this vital centre the world and its ways are the whole object of attention. The mind is set upon earth. Consider another passage in the Bible in which Paul reveals why the world is under the wrath of God (Rom. 1: 18–32). What is his emphasis? Men 'suppress the truth' (verse 18); 'although they knew God they did not honour him as God' (verse 21); they 'became futile in their thinking' (verse 21); 'they exchanged the truth about God' (verse 25); 'they did not see fit to acknowledge God' (verse 28); 'God gave them up to a base mind' (verse 28). The point of spiritual collapse came in the place where men *know*, grasp *truth*, *reason*, make up the *mind*. The rebellion of the mind from God is the fundamental state of the sinner. Turn now to other passages in which Paul reveals the life of regeneration: 'be transformed by the renewal of your mind' (Rom. 12: 2); 'be renewed in the spirit of your minds' (Eph. 4: 23); 'Set your minds on things that are above' (Col. 3: 2). What a vital part the mind plays in the experience of the Christian! We need wonder no longer why Paul will presently say to the Philippians, 'whatever is true . . . honourable . . . just . . . pure . . . lovely . . . gracious . . . *think* about these things' (4:8). The voice of the wise man advised, 'Keep your heart with all vigilance; for from it flow the springs of life' (Pr. 4: 23). The mind astray from God is the most potent of all forces for spiritual disaster. Paul has raised his warning again. Here is the downward path, and those who walk on it are enemies of the cross of Christ.

III REMEDY

What, in brief, will describe these people? They are 'enemies of the cross of Christ'. They are heading for perdition because they have set themselves against the only way of salvation; they worship their own selves because they have refused to worship God their Saviour; they live by perverted values because they do not accept the moral code inculcated by Calvary; their mind is on the earth because they have never been transformed by the power of His redeeming grace.

But this means that the cross is the remedy for the disease of degeneration. When Paul faithfully raises his warning sign against the pathway that leads to perdition, he also lifts up the cross as the emblem of the pathway that leads to life. It is clear that

Paul expects contemplation of the cross to produce the opposite of the symptoms of degeneration, the starkly contrasting apostolic life. If they are the people who are enemies of the cross, should not we be those who love it—or rather Him who died upon it? We ought to find in the cross and the crucified Christ the solution to bodily temptations, spiritual discernment for daily life and decisions, and power for the inner transformation of mind and heart. The question therefore is inescapable at the conclusion of our study: do we know the cross well enough and deeply enough for it to produce these desirable fruits in us?

21 CHRIST OUR HOPE

THE BIBLE IS A GREAT BOOK FOR INSISTING on living in the present: '*Now* is the day of salvation' (2 Cor. 6: 2). But it never draws a foolish line between past, present, and future in this regard. Successful life in the present takes account of the lessons and blessings of the past, and of the demands and prospects of the future. Consequently, in this present passage, Paul has already shown that life lived in the apostolic mould rests upon the past event of Calvary. It is a proper relation to and love for the cross of Christ which rescues us from the danger of spiritual degeneration. But equally we must have that forward look which was such a characteristic of the New Testament. Did the apostles believe that Christ would come back in their lifetime? Of course they did! No other attitude is permitted to the New Testament Christian!

This is the doctrine that has so largely been forgotten—even where it is not denied altogether—by the contemporary church. And very often in those sections of the church where it is still held and studied, the joy of the Lord's return is lost in controversies and speculations of the most complicated nature. Paul has a word for all in these present verses. Those who have forgotten the Lord's coming again will find here a thrilling reminder of it. Those who have almost lost sight of the coming Saviour amid the complexities of theories about when and where and how, will be recalled to the bare and glorious essential, that *He* will come again. Those who dismiss such a doctrine—for whatever reason—must face here an apostolic reaffirmation of it in the most unequivocal and unmistakable terms.

I A DISTINCTIVE CHRISTIAN BELIEF

In the last study we saw how the life and prospects of the enemies of the cross of Christ contrasted diametrically, point by point, with the personal life and hopes of Paul as displayed in his pattern life. In verse 20, where he turns to speak of the hope that is common to all Christians, he naturally changes from the 'I' of testimony to the 'we' of shared truth. But again, and as if deliberately, he points up the contrast between the 'enemies' and those with whom he identifies himself.

The 'enemies of the cross' are heading for 'destruction' (verse 19), but we for salvation (verse 20) for we are waiting for 'a Saviour' from heaven. They are devoted to the body, worshipping and making a god of its appetites, but we, quite the reverse, look for its transformation, for we consider it to be 'our lowly body', literally 'the body of our humiliation' (verse 21). They have a perverted, topsy-turvy scale of values, glorying in shameful things, but we possess a true perception of value, having some appreciation even now of His glory (verse 21). And finally, they are earthbound, while 'our commonwealth is in heaven' (verse 20).

Thus the contrast is complete, but the description—or the implied description—is unexpected. They are 'enemies of the cross of Christ', and we would naturally expect that when the apostle so concisely describes the opposite sort of people he would call them 'lovers, or friends of the cross of Christ'—and how true and exact that description would be, for all the distinctive features wherein we differ from the 'enemies' are Calvary-based! But he does not do so. He describes us as 'watchers for the return'—'we await a Saviour'.

This parity of the cross and the return is surprising. Is it not true to say that we think of the cross as a cardinal Christian doctrine to a degree that we do not usually accord to the second coming? But Paul makes the two events equally the basis of present Christian living. Indeed the more one studies these verses the more it becomes apparent that Paul could equally well have described the 'enemies' as hostile to the Lord's return and Christians as living on the basis of His past work of salvation on the cross.

The return of Christ, then, is a distinctive Christian doctrine and cannot be jettisoned from our statement of faith if we are to learn from the New Testament. We must learn, in fact, to think in God's way. We have been taught already that 'he who began a good work in you' is continually completing it with a view to 'the day of Jesus Christ'. The second coming is the designed end of all God's saving work. Again we have been taught that the death of Christ has been the subject of deliberate divine appraisal and response. God has responded to the cross (2: 8) in the supreme exaltation of Jesus above every conceivable authority (2: 9-11), and the intended outcome of this is universal submission to Jesus Christ who is Lord. In God's estimation Calvary requires the return as its only just and adequate acknowledgment. Nothing else will suffice to express what God thinks of the obedience to death of His Son. To deny the return is to fail to appreciate the cross; to forget the return is to lose hold of the excellence of the cross.

II THE CHRISTIAN'S PERSONAL LONGING

Because he has this awareness of the return of Christ as an essential and distinctive Christian belief, equal in importance to Calvary, Paul confidently expects that all Christians will be one with him in looking for it expectantly. He speaks, therefore, of 'we' (verses 20,21). What is this expectation?

First, we may note a longing for the blessings which the returning Christ will bring with Him. Very practically Paul puts his finger on the point of our present need, 'our lowly body' (verse 21). It is no wonder that he had to warn us so strongly of the power of the example of those whose 'god is the belly'. For Christians are constantly aware of the downward pull of their bodily members. Here is a constant point of Christian shortcoming and failure: the uncontrolled lust, the unmanageable tongue, the laziness which keeps us out of bed too late at night and in bed too late in the morning, the 'unwilling flesh' which clogs the ambitions of the 'willing spirit' (*cf.* Mk. 14: 38; Rom. 7: 18–24)—and this is not to mention the gradual failing of bodily strength with the passing years so that the mental powers wane and understanding diminishes, or the debilitating and often humiliating aspects of illness, or failing sight, or any of the other numerous ways in which the body holds us back and keeps us down—truly 'our lowly body'.

But here is hope of One who will 'change our lowly body to be like his glorious body'. The pattern of this refashioning was elsewhere described by Paul as the continuation of personal identity in the midst of a most remarkable alteration: the seed growing into its own characteristic flower (1 Cor. 15: 35–49). What a humble thing a seed is—unimpressive, unattractive, unpromising to all outward appearance! Yet *this* seed becomes *that* flower! Continuity and transformation! So it will be for our loved ones who are already with the Lord, and we shall know them when we see them for there is continuity within the glory that is now theirs; so it shall be with us who love His cross and His coming.

This transformed body will be the perfect vehicle of the new nature. In the word 'to be like' (RV 'conformed') Paul uses virtually the same word which taught that Christ Jesus was in the 'form' of God (2: 6). The word points to the perfect outward expression of the inner nature and character of the person concerned. When the returning Lord bestows on us a body 'like his glorious body' it is not only that we shall be like Him (*cf.* 1 Jn. 3: 2) but that this glorious outward appearance will be the perfect reflection of and vehicle for the expression of a nature fully perfected, the new nature of the Christian brought to completion.

But this longing for the blessings He brings is derivative. The real longing expressed here is for Christ Himself, 'we await a Saviour, the Lord Jesus Christ.' The verb expresses a concentrated eagerness and perseverance of hope; it suggests that the eye looks for nothing else but the sight of the returning Lord and never wearies in looking, so great is the yearning to see Him (*cf.* Gal. 5: 5; Rom. 8: 25; Heb. 9: 28). He comes in His office as Saviour —here again is the intimate association of the coming with the cross—and in the fullness of His divine-human Person, 'the Lord Jesus Christ'. Indeed, we can catch some sense of Paul's longing to see Him by the fact that (so to speak) he cannot bear to leave out any item in the full title of his Saviour—'the Lord Jesus Christ'. It is He who stands as the supremely attractive element in the Christian hope. We look forward to many things: deliverance from temptation; meeting the great ones of old—Abraham, David, Isaiah, Paul—what a place heaven will be!—reunion with our own loved ones; the glory of the heavenly places.

Yes, indeed, all these things, but beyond them all that one feature which gives coherence and meaning and focus to heaven, that one Person through whom alone this great company is gathered and for whom alone is the glory, 'the Lamb standing, as though it had been slain' (Rev. 5: 6), 'the Lamb in the midst of the throne' (Rev. 7: 17), the 'Saviour, the Lord Jesus Christ'. 'So shall we always be *with the Lord*' wrote Paul in another place (1 Thes. 4: 17). 'His servants shall worship him; they shall see his face', promised John (Rev. 22: 4):

The bride eyes not her garments
But her dear Bridegroom's face;
I will not gaze on glory,
But on my King of grace:
Not on the crown He giveth,
But His own pierced hand;
The Lamb is all the glory
In Immanuel's Land.

III A GUARANTEED CERTAINTY

No argument against the possibility of the second coming can survive against the teaching of these verses. Here indeed is that which deserves the description 'hope', for in the New Testament there is no uncertainty in hope but guaranteed occurrence at an unspecified time. Paul offers no dates for the return of Christ. It is both an imminent possibility for which the Christian must be in constant readiness (*cf.* 4: 2–6), and it is capable of tarrying for a thousand years (*cf.* 2 Pet. 3: 3–10). But nothing can stop it happening at the moment which God the Father has foreordained for it (Mk. 13: 32; Acts 1: 7).

The guarantee is expressed here in the words 'by the power which enables him even to subject all things to himself' (verse 21). The ability of the Lord is stated in three ways here. First, it is His inherent ability, 'which enables him'. The same Greek word has contributed 'dynamite' to English. 'He is dynamite'! This belongs by right and by nature to the Lord Jesus. But many people have natural capacities which they have no authority to make use of or to apply to life. Before he became Prime Minister the late Winston

Churchill possessed all the qualities of leadership, decision, and action which he later displayed, but they were dormant in him for he had no opportunity to apply them and make them work. Thus Paul takes his description of the 'dynamic' of the Lord Jesus and describes it in another way. It is working 'power'. This is the same word which we know as 'energy' and it is used in the New Testament to describe the power of God effectually at work, accomplishing His will. Thus, in 2: 13, 'God is at work (is energizing) in you'—the effectual operation of divine power within the believer. Jesus then not only possesses inherent power but also power to act. His power is both inherent and applied. Thirdly, it is invincible, for it is the applied power 'which enables him *even to subject all things* to himself'. 'To subject all things': the 'forces' of nature, the ordered universe, the unbelieving hearts of men, the spiritual wickedness in heavenly places, the prince of the power of the air. Say what you will of opponents of the return of Christ and Paul will nullify their opposition with this triple definition of the ability of the returning Lord: His power is inherent, applied, and invincible, and it is this power which underwrites the promise of His coming again.

IV PRESENT IMPLICATIONS

The Bible never foretells the future in order to satisfy the 'horoscope' tendencies of the human mind. We have an immense curiosity as to 'what will happen next'. The promise of the second coming is given without date so that we may now live as those who expect *today* to meet their Lord (*cf.* Lk. 12: 35–48). Life in the present is motivated by awareness of the future.

Let us notice therefore how Paul begins his description of the *future* hope of the Christian with a sentence in the *present* tense. 'Our commonwealth (RV, 'citizenship') *is* in heaven.' The verb 'to be' in that sentence is a translation of a word expressing that which belongs to a person as a natural possession, as in the phrase 'these men *are* Jews' (Acts 16: 20): that is to say, they are Jews by nature; that is their proper and inalienable status. So, says Paul, Christians have a natural, proper, and inalienable status as citizens in the commonwealth of heaven. That is their present position; that is their status now as they await the Saviour from heaven. They belong to a far-off homeland and they are waiting with longing expectation for the King of that land to come and fetch them.

The word 'citizenship' (RV, *cf.* RSV, 'commonwealth') would have made splendid sense at Philippi, for, along with their status as a 'colony' (Acts 16: 12), 'citizenship' went as a privilege. That is to say, their names were inscribed on the citizenship rolls at Rome (*cf.* 4: 3), and, though far off from their 'home', yet they could live in Philippi and, indeed, were expected to live in Philippi in the enjoyment of the same privileges which would be theirs if they moved to Rome itself. Thus 'our commonwealth is in heaven', and our present status is that of citizens of heaven. Our names are on the rolls there. We must live now (while we wait for our King) in the enjoyment of the privileges which would be ours if we moved there and which will be ours when He fetches us there.

These are the present implications of His coming, that when He comes He should find us enjoying the rights and fulfilling the duties of citizens. In the heavenly homeland, the primary feature is His personal presence. Very well, then, as citizens that is the privilege of our present daily life. Let us realize it and enjoy it and live in the awareness that He is with us. In the heavenly homeland, all are conformed to His likeness; let us 'occupy till he comes' in becoming 'like him in his death; that if possible I may attain the resurrection of the dead' (3: 10,11). In the heavenly homeland, all things are ordered by His almighty, all-subduing power. This power is now at work in us (2: 13; Eph. 3: 20) and is available to us for the living out of the life which accords with His desires for us and which He displayed for our learning in the pattern life of Paul.

22 MEANWHILE

PAUL DOES NOT NEED ANY HELP in drawing conclusions! We ventured to end the preceding study by suggesting the present implications of the sure hope of the Lord's return, and, arising out of a proper understanding of the idea of commonwealth membership, those conclusions were correct. We need to be careful, however, not to allow our necessary and right desire to know the implications of what Scripture says to draw our attention away from any such practical conclusions as Scripture itself may draw. And here, without withdrawing the teaching of citizenship inherent in 3: 20,21, we find ourselves faced with Paul's own 'therefore' (4: 1). He will now tell us how to live in the meantime between Calvary and the coming.

At Philippi they were facing two distinct situations, and we have surely learned by now that we are in no whit different from them. Paul is addressing us. We do not have to stick rigidly to past tenses, 'Paul said, wrote, taught'. Indeed it would be a denial of the nature of Scripture and of the role of the apostle if we did. We must read the Epistle to the Philippians as sent to us. We must use present tenses, 'Paul says, writes, teaches', for he is the Lord's messenger to us and to our circumstances. First, then, he sees the need to 'stand firm' (verse 1) and we can only understand this as requiring a resolute facing of opponents. The Philippians were in the midst of 'enemies', basically 'enemies of the cross of Christ' but equally enemies of the true spiritual well-being of each Christian. Paul gives the impression in 3: 17,18 of a present, persistent, persuasive foe. There is real danger of the Christian being drawn away; there is real pressure upon the church. Consequently there is need to 'stand firm', to lay hold on the powers rightfully theirs in their heavenly citizenship and to pursue the life which pleases God (3: 15).

Alongside this there was the practical need for unity in the local church (verses 2,3). Christians cannot stand fast from a position of division and disharmony. 'All one in Christ Jesus' must be a reality in the local community of believers, and, once more, we are made to feel the apostle's sense of outrage at divisions between Christians. Just as we sense the greatness of God's abhorrence of sin when we realize that Isaiah felt himself to be ruined because of slips of the tongue (Is. 6: 5)—a matter which we very often do not reckon to be sinful at all!—so we sense here the apostle's antagonism to division between Christians when we realize that he gives specific mention to two otherwise unknown women, Euodia and Syntyche, and tells them to settle their difference. Was some great doctrinal issue at stake? We are not told, but it is most unlikely. No, two women had fallen out, and Paul feels that a solemn and indeed disastrous thing has happened.

In the first place, such divisions are *contrary to the apostle's mind*. His attitude towards other Christians is expressed in his address to them in verse 1, 'my brethren, whom I love and long for, my joy and crown . . . my beloved'. If this is the way Christians should view each other, then division is scandal indeed, for we must remember that apostolic achievements are Christian ideals (*cf*. 3: 15,17; 4: 9). Christians belong in a family unity: to Paul, they are 'my brethren'. It was a triumph of grace that this should have been so. Paul was the proud Pharisee, with an intense awareness both of his own privileged status and of the Gentile's, not just lack of privilege, but positive rejection. In Ephesians 2: 12 he gives a factual description of the Gentile case: 'separated from Christ, alienated from the commonwealth of Israel, and strangers to the covenants of promise, having no hope and without God in the world'. If we subtract all Paul's missionary enthusiasm from this verse and all his love and longing for the lost, and put in their place an acceptance of a *status quo* for the Gentiles, and even a certain satisfaction that it should be thus with them, we have some idea of the gulf between Jew and non-Jew in the ancient world. But now, in Christ, they are brothers; all are in one family (*cf*. Eph. 2: 18 ff.); they have a Father, and a Saviour, and a Comforter in common. The division of Christians is the sin of fratricide.

Tender affection is the next element in the apostle's attitude towards his fellow Christians: 'Whom I love and long for . . . beloved'. The repetition underlines the emotion. He really loves them! 'This is my beloved Son', said God (Mt. 3: 17), and Paul does not hesitate to use the same word of his feeling towards his fellow-believers. (*Cf*. the repeated 'beloved' in RV.) But he adds to it a word of even greater intensity, 'long for'. He used it previously of his longing for the Philippians in 1: 8, and gave it a very characteristic setting in the case of Epaphroditus (2: 26) who, he says, was 'longing for them all', or 'was home-sick'. We need not develop the idea any further. To put it just like that rebukes our lukewarm affection for our fellow Christians. We have a long way to go before we are feeling the emotions of Christ towards each other as Paul was (*cf*. 1: 8)—we who so easily dismiss from our reckoning those whom God has accepted and reconciled (*cf*. Rom. 14: 3), and who so lightly offend those for whom Christ died (*cf*. Rom. 14: 15–20). If we felt for each other as Paul did, we would soon recognize the scandal of division.

But he also went one step further. Other Christians were to him the objects of pastoral concern, 'my joy and crown'. When Paul thus uses these words he has his mind fixed on the day of Christ and our gathering together to Him (*cf*. for his joy, 2: 16–18; and for 'joy and crown', 1 Thes. 2: 19). It is part of Paul's love for his Christian friends that he longs for them to be ready and to be acceptable to Christ on the day of His return. The 'crown' to which he refers can be equally that of 'victor or of holiday-maker' (Lightfoot). To Paul it is a victory to see them accepted before the throne, and at the same time the proper garland of one who is banqueting with the King of kings and His chosen guests. Thus, in part, his zealous and affectionate concern for them is explained. He sees them in the light of Calvary where they were purchased and of the coming by which they will be gathered into glory.

On all these counts, therefore, division scandalized Paul. It was the very reverse of his apostolic mind. But equally, a divided church is a contradiction in another way: it is *contrary to the nature of the church*. Incidentally to verse 3, in which Paul summons certain other Christians to the aid of the quarrelling women, we see what the church would be like were it true to its nature. Of the three truths about the church found here the first is that the church possesses *a single task*, 'they have laboured side by side with me in the gospel' or 'they and I were co-workers in the gospel'. Where there is agreement as to what the gospel is and what ought to be done with it there is no room left for personal disagreement. The one ought to exclude the other. Very often, of course, as at Philippi, it does not; but it ought to. To agree on the gospel is the most fundamental form of unity: it involves a unity of mind and heart as to the doctrine and personal experience of salvation. To agree as to what the gospel demands in its proclamation to the world is to cement unity by common action. The singleness of the task ought to be reflected in the singleness of the workers.

Furthermore, the church should be marked by *mutual helpfulness,* 'Help these women.' The word used points to 'taking hold along with'. It is as though Paul said, 'They are carrying a burden —admittedly a burden of their own devising, a burden of animosity and bitterness. Take hold of it with them and help them to cast it off.' No Christian, we might say, is at liberty to stand aloof from the needs of any other Christian. The very existence of the need is of itself a call to come to the rescue. Paul does not say to Euodia and Syntyche that they should ask the 'true yokefellow' for his help. The command is to him to make common cause (uninvited, save by Paul) with them. We do not know who this person was. Some have suggested that the translation should be 'Synzygos, well-named'—a man who by name and nature was a 'yokefellow'. But maybe Paul is summoning Christians in general to the rescue of the troubled women, 'If any of you would live up to your place and duty as Christians, take this yoke on you and help the women out of their tangled life.' Maybe so, we cannot say; but we can say that this element of mutual assistance was assumed by Paul as proper to inter-Christian relationships.

Finally, Paul displays the church as a place of *fundamental oneness,* 'whose names are in the book of life'. There is a heavenly reality about the church, and there are no divisions in heaven. All who are there are 'one in Christ Jesus', for none enter that kingdom but those who 'have washed their robes and made them white in the blood of the Lamb' (Rev. 7: 14) and their security of tenure depends on their names being in 'the Lamb's book of life' (Rev. 20: 12–14; 21: 27). Divisions contradict this fundamental 'fact of life'. The church on earth is called to be a replica of the ideal or heavenly. This is involved, as we saw so clearly, in the possession of heavenly citizenship: to live here and now in enjoyment of the privileges and practice of the duties of the far-off homeland. Thus it is against the nature of the church, the community of the redeemed (Acts 20: 28), to confess unity in heaven and practise disunity on earth.

In this incidental polemic against disunity and division, Paul reminds us thirdly of the practical point, that division among Christians is *a serious flaw in the church's armour against the world.* In order to see this we must observe that for the second time Paul is allowing his thoughts to travel along the same line. In 1: 27 he called the church to 'stand firm in one Spirit' for he discerned that there were 'opponents' (1: 28) whose opposition could easily 'stampede' the Christians in terror. Here again, in 4: 1, the call goes forth to 'stand firm . . . in the Lord' for once more Paul has descried 'enemies of the cross' whose pernicious example could draw the Christians away from apostolic ways and into paths of spiritual danger. But he developed his exhortation in the earlier place by showing that only a united church could present a united front, resolutely facing opposition and not giving ground. Therefore in 2: 2 he required them to be 'of the same mind'. Equally in 4: 2 the requirement of unity is made, 'Agree in the Lord.' The parallelism of thought is more than striking. Twice over Paul takes the same line, that only a united church can hope to face its foes and stand firm. Where there is disharmony within there is bound to be defeat without. Where Christians cannot bear the sight of each other they will not be able to look the world in the face either. They cannot win on the vital 'front' of their contact with the world if they are secretly carrying on warfare on a 'second front' of their own devising.

In summary, then, this is why Paul sees disunity as such a solemn and disastrous thing: it is contrary to the apostolic mind; it is a denial of the nature of the church; and it is a flaw in the church's armour against the world. In the light of all this, how noteworthy that Paul (who apparently knew all about the differences between the two ladies in question) neither specifies the problem nor tries to act as a mediator. He does not attempt any judicious summing up of their rival claims; he does not say to the one or to the other, 'You are in the wrong; you must apologize.' He does not temporize with a conventional sitting on the fence, 'There is right and wrong on both sides, so please kiss and be friends.' To him, divisions are such a scandal that the ladies are equally exhorted ('I entreat . . . I entreat. . . . ') to be their own best friends and have done with their arguings.

And even to this day we do not know what their quarrel was about. Surely this was by Paul's deliberate purpose. By leaving out the sordid local details he presents us with a general—and all too common situation. There is division and disharmony in the local church. Whether it is 'serious'—*i.e.* on a point of major teaching or policy—or whether it is trivial, two quarrelling women who 'happen' to get on each other's nerves—it is a blot on the church's record and a major disease. By not specifying their quarrel Paul makes his teaching relevant to all quarrels. Where there is division between Christians it must cease. It has no place in the church.

23 THE PEACE OF GOD AND THE GOD OF PEACE

PUBLIC PROBLEMS REQUIRE PRIVATE SOLUTIONS. We have already traced out the parallel between Paul's teaching from 1: 27 to 2: 2 and his teaching from 3: 18 to 4: 2. In each case he was insistent that only a united church can face the world without retreating. But the parallel between the two sections goes one step further. In 2: 2–4, when tackling the problem of a divided church, he focused his teaching upon the individual Christian, 'each of you' (verse 4). In the last analysis therefore the public success of the church along the front where it faces the world depends upon the measure of sanctification of each individual Christian.

The teaching is precisely the same, though differently expressed and developed, in the later passage which now lies before us. For in calling out for unity and unanimity within the local church fellowship, Paul starts with the individuals who are disaffected, Euodia and Syntyche (verse 2), but then he proceeds with a general exhortation to all individuals. He uses plural verbs, 'Rejoice', *etc.*, but the command is common rather than corporate, for his point of conclusion is 'your hearts and your minds' (verse 7)—the inward state of the individual church members. We shall study his teaching under three headings: the needs, the promises, and the conditions.

I THE NEEDS

At the risk of being tedious, let us try to see again the structure of this passage. It presents precisely the same pattern which we found in 1: 27–2: 4. Again we have an inverted triangle with the long side uppermost and the point at the bottom. The long side represents the frontier where church and world face each other: the 'enmity' of 3: 18. The point on which the church is supported for the conflict is the individual believer—the 'hearts and minds' of 4: 7. The needs of this believer in the parallel passage in 1: 27–2: 4 were those characteristics of glad self-submission and obedience to the will of God which were exemplified in Christ (2: 5–8). But as Paul analyses the individual's needs here he sees him to require reassurance at two points: verse 7, 'the peace of God . . . will keep your hearts and your minds', and verse 9, 'the God of peace will be with you.'

First, there is the need of a garrison (for this is the meaning of the word 'guard') around 'hearts and minds'. We have already referred to the passages of Scripture which will enable us to understand why Paul sees this as the primary Christian need. 'Hearts and minds' point to source and outflow. The source is the 'heart', that comprehensive term which the Bible uses to include functions which we would distribute between mind, will, emotions, and conscience. It is the inner side of the personality, and in particular the inner source from which all outer life springs. The 'mind' is the outflow from this source in terms of definite plans which we entertain, imaginations which captivate us, and so forth. Now, the 'heart' in this sense has much the same meaning as 'mind' in 3: 19, the inner source and spring of life, and as we saw there it is the mind astray from God which is the cause of man's downfall and the primary object of God's wrath (referring to Rom. 1 : 18 ff.), and it is the mind renewed in Christ which is the growing-point of the new life of the child of God (referring to Rom. 12: 2, *etc.*). Since, therefore, the outward impact of the church upon the world depends upon its own inward unity, member to member, and since this in turn depends upon sanctified individuals, the first and most crying need is for a transformation and keeping of 'hearts and minds in Christ Jesus' lest they go the way of the 'enemies of the cross of Christ' and individual degeneration bring the cause of the gospel into jeopardy.

Hard on the heels of this need Paul mentions another: the need for the conscious presence of God: verse 9, 'the God of peace will be with you'. Why should he make this promise unless in response to a discerned need? But why does he discern it? It may be that he is balancing any wrong deduction that might be drawn from the teaching on the return of Christ in 3: 20,21. It might justly be said that one of the marks of this age of the church is the absence of Christ. He is not here; He is risen. Nevertheless, the position of the church and of the believer is not only that of one waiting for an absent Lord to return; it is also that of one enjoying the presence of a Lord who is still here, though invisible. But this doctrine, though true, has its own peculiar danger: the presence of God can so easily become, as it were, a credal formula rather than a living experience, a tangible reality. While we (theoretically) know that He is with us, we can at the same time (experimentally) forget Him! And in the absence of a vivid sense of the presence of God we can easily fall into sins and slackness which a potent realization of His companionship would banish from our conduct and even from our desires. Hence the need to know that in truth and reality the God of peace is *with us.*

II THE PROMISES

Against this background of individual needs, Paul paints in very vividly three satisfying promises. They are expressed in the three phrases, 'which passes all understanding', 'the peace of God . . . will keep', and 'the God of peace will be with you'.

The first promise is that our lives will be touched with the evidence of the supernatural, 'the peace of God, *which passes all understanding*', which 'transcends all power of conception' (Lightfoot), 'beyond the range of our comprehension' (Martin). Much of our difficulty in 'standing firm' in the face of a hostile world is that people do not see why we want (as they say) to be different. The world puts our attempt to live by different standards down to personal whim or fancy. It looks upon us as rather in the category of the lady whose recent obituary notice remarked that 'her chief hobby was religion'. One man cleans the car on Sunday while his neighbour attends church, but it is all a matter of preference. What the church and the individual believer needs more than anything today, as at every other period of history, is the touch of the supernatural, something that cannot be explained except by saying, 'This is the finger of God' (Ex.

8: 19). Paul expressed the same truth when he asserted that Christians can be 'super-conquerors' (Rom. 8: 37), that is, can so rise above the challenge of life that it can be explained only by appeal to the power of God at work in them. Again, in calling Christians to live 'as in the day' (Rom. 13: 13), he not only asked for different standards of behaviour but also for a 'putting on' of the Lord Jesus Christ. Once more his great desire was that there should be something about Christians which the world could not explain in its own categories and would be compelled to admit as the work of God. Hence, here, a peace 'which passes all understanding' is positively promised. It 'will keep your hearts'.

The second promise is of guardianship and companionship, 'The peace of God . . . will keep . . . the God of peace will be with you.' We will not go wrong if we take this to be the picture of a besieged citadel. It is the castle of the mind of the Christian. If it can be held, progress in sanctification and renewal goes forward; if it can be captured, then backsliding and spiritual decadence begins. But it is garrisoned strongly. Its walls are constantly patrolled. Its sentries never sleep at their posts. The troops are the Household Guards of the King of kings and they march behind the standard of the peace of God. Meanwhile, inside the citadel hearts and thoughts alike are kept in quietness for their Companion is the King Himself, the 'God of peace' who is with them. Whether or not Paul had such a picture in mind, this is the upshot of his words: the presence of God in power and in experience.

The third promise is peace, 'the peace of God . . . the God of peace. . . .' Detached from its New Testament content, the word peace is a sort of spiritual marshmallow, full of softness and sweetness but without much actual substance. But if we study the scriptures which associate peace and God it is surprisingly full of strength and vigour. The 'God of peace' is the God who makes peace between Himself and sinners. Thus peace is linked with God's work of salvation. For example, when the risen Christ visited His disciples in the locked upper room on the first Easter evening His word to them was, 'Peace be with you' (Jn. 20 : 19) and this was no conventional greeting, for He repeated it almost at once, 'Peace be with you' (verse 21) as if to underline a surprising and splendid reality. John does well to link the word of 'peace' with Christ's showing of His hands and side (verse 20), for peace is the first-fruit of Calvary for the sinner. The God of peace, therefore, is the God of salvation, the God who is not defeated by sin but does away with sin by the offering of His Son upon the cross (Heb. 10: 10–14).

The God of peace is also the God of power, for it is 'the God of peace who brought again from the dead our Lord Jesus, the great shepherd of the sheep, by the blood of the eternal covenant' (Heb. 13: 20), and the resurrection is the standard New Testament demonstration of divine might (Eph. 1: 19,20). Peace is thus associated with power, such power that not even death is strong enough to stand against the God of peace.

Another passage teaches us that the 'God of peace will soon crush Satan under your feet' (Rom. 16: 20). Thus, once again, peace is not a vague feeling of well-being. The God of peace is the God of victory against whom not even Satan can stand. The promise of peace, therefore, is as comprehensive as we could find, for it is the promise of salvation, power and victory all in one. God places the individual Christian in the place of the most demanding responsibility. Each of us must consider that the forward march and the resolute stand of the church in the world depends directly upon the state of my heart, the quality of my holiness. This is indeed true and Paul has said it twice over lest we should miss it. In this situation God is not simply the setter of an example (2: 5–8) but also the mighty indwelling Worker (2: 13). Furthermore He is the God who will set His supernatural mark upon our lives, be both our Guard and our Companion, and bestow upon us His peace which holds in one embrace His gift of salvation, His almighty power, and His irresistible conquest. If it is true that we are called to a great and frightening task, is it not equally and even more true that the equipment promised is sufficient?

III THE CONDITIONS

These great promises are all contained in verses 7 and 9, and in reading the verses in order to dwell upon the promises we have hitherto left out one most important word which they have in common, the word 'and'. Verse 7 does not say, 'The peace of God . . . will keep your hearts.' It says, '*And* the peace. . . .' Likewise verse 9 does not say, 'The God of peace will be with you.' It says, '*and* the God of peace will be with you'. That is to say, the promises are consequent upon something else which has been stated previously. When we look to see what that 'something else' is, we find a series of commands in each case, so that the Word of God is saying to us that if we want the promises to be fulfilled then we must exercise ourselves in obedience to the commands. The promises are ours on certain specified conditions. These may be stated as four distinct *laws*.

First, there is *a law for our relationships*, the centrality of the Lord Jesus Christ: 'Rejoice in the Lord always. . . . Let all men know your forbearance. The Lord is at hand' (verses 4,5). Glorying in Christ Jesus was the central feature of the religion of the covenant people of God (3: 3), and this was but another way of saying 'rejoice in the Lord' (3: 1). The essence of the matter is so to value Jesus Christ, and so to long for the smile of His approval that nothing else matters. He is all our joy. And naturally in the present context, we cannot hope to enjoy the peace of God if we give less than the first place to Him who is our peace (Eph. 2: 14). But this is not in fact the main thrust of Paul's command. When he says here that we are to 'rejoice in the Lord' he continues by urging us to imitate Him in our behaviour in expectancy of His coming, 'Let all men know your (gentle) forbearance. The Lord is at hand.' It must be that Paul is looking back to the example of Christ which so occupied him when earlier he was exhorting the individual to sanctified relationships (2: 5–8). He sums up the Lord's attitude towards others in the lovely word which we have translated as 'gentle forbearance', the uncomplaining readiness to accept others as they are and to submit oneself to their demands. Such was Christ, and such must be those who claim to rejoice only in Him: all the more so in that He is near, His coming is at hand. How *He* will rejoice *in us* if He finds *us* so rejoicing *in Him* that we are content to be like Him!

Secondly, there is *a law for our circumstances,* the antidote of prayer: 'Have no anxiety about anything, but in everything by prayer and supplication with thanksgiving let your requests be made known to God' (verse 6). Paul offers here a timeless and universal remedy for anxiety: 'Have no anxiety . . . but in everything. . . .' Prayer is both the antidote to anxiety, and the prelude to the enjoyment of peace, because prayer expresses *trust,* and thanksgiving expresses *acceptance* of our circumstances from God, and together prayer and thanksgiving commit us into the keeping of the sovereign God who is in charge of our lives, and in His care we find peace. Of the words used here, 'prayer' is general, the bringing of the matter to God; 'supplication' points to the statement of our *needs* before God; and 'requests' means the itemizing or detailing before Him of the things we ask (*cf.* Lk. 18: 41). This is the law for our circumstances and the direct way of peace at all times.

Thirdly, Paul lays down *a law for our thoughts,* the discipline of the mind: 'whatever is true . . . think about these things' (verse 8). We need not open again the subject of the cardinal place occupied by the mind for both good and ill. A carnal mind is the surest and most direct passport to the downward path; likewise a mind drilled to dwell upon things which have divine approval is the surest and steadiest way of newness of life. The allowable and profitable objects for our mental concentration are those which are *true, honourable* (that is, worthy of honour or inviting respect), *just,* (morally) *pure, lovely* (in the sense of exciting genuine and proper admiration), *of good report* (or 'bringing with them a good report', commendable), and anything properly deserving the name of *virtue* or qualifying for God's *praise.* 'Think about these things'—that is to say, 'take them into account, reflect upon them, and allow them to condition your whole way of life' (Martin). The mind must be held on course. It is the will of God that by giving our attention to things of which He approves we should shape our minds into the likeness of His.

Fourthly, we find here *a law for our behaviour,* the authority of the Word of God: 'What you have learned and received and heard and seen in me, do' (verse 9). If we are to know the presence of the God of peace then, for certain, we must seek the life of which He approves. 'God will reveal that also to you', said Paul, referring to his own apostolic example (3:15). In Paul there was a perfect dovetailing of precept and example ('heard and seen'); in Paul there resided that apostolic authority whereby he could require the acceptance of what he taught ('received'). For us, who no longer have Paul, nor any apostle, the commandment comes in the form of a requirement to submit to the apostolic word, the continuing apostolate of Holy Scripture in the Christian church.

These, then, are the laws, or preconditions, for enjoying the promises of God. If we are, as a church, to stand fast in the face of the world, then we must give primary attention to the inner quality of our personal sanctification, the state of the individual heart and thoughts. If, however, we are to enjoy the power of God at work in our inner being, then we must give attention to these outward laws which God imposes upon us—relationships modelled upon Christ, circumstances surrounded by prayer, the mind drilled in godly thinking, and the life subjected to the Word of God. Let these things be so, '*and* the peace of God, which passes all understanding, will keep . . . hearts and . . . minds in Christ Jesus . . . *and* the God of peace will be with you'. If we ignore the laws we must be prepared to forgo the blessings.

24 THE CONTENTED CHRISTIAN

IT IS EASIER TO BE A CHRISTIAN at some times than at others. Ask a preacher whether he is more zealous for the Lord on Saturdays, when the responsibility of Sunday's preaching is holding him to the highest, or on Monday morning when 'the fight is o'er'! Circumstances sometimes press us closer to the Lord and sometimes conspire to edge us away from Him, and for all of us, at some time or another, in ways great or small, the bell rings when we hear our Lord warn that 'when tribulation or persecution arises on account of the word, immediately they fall away' (Mk. 4: 17).

None of these things moved Paul. As he turns to autobiography in these closing verses of the Epistle, he is the man of unshakable contentment. Do his circumstances vary from one extreme to the other? Then 'in any and all circumstances I have learned the secret of facing plenty and hunger, abundance and want' (verse 12). Has he received a helpful gift from the Philippian church? Then, whatever they sent contents him, 'I have received full payment, and more; I am filled' (verse 18). Does he face an uncertain future? Then 'I can do *all things* in him who strengthens me' (verse 13).

Here indeed is Christian contentment. As Paul testifies to his contentedness, he shows that three factors contributed to his mastery of variable circumstances.

I CHRISTIAN GENEROSITY

Paul had a sufficiency because other Christians contributed to his necessity, and he was glad to acknowledge his indebtedness (verses 10,14,15,16,18). Thus he enunciates a principle: *the sufficiency of one Christian is related to the generosity of another*. Or, if we may rephrase this principle in the light of the fact that 'every good endowment and every perfect gift is from above' (Jas. 1: 17), then we must say that *the Lord uses Christian generosity to meet Christian needs* (*cf.* 2 Cor. 8: 1–15, especially verses 13–15).

Such generosity towards Paul was *an ever-present sentiment* among the Philippians. 'You were indeed concerned for me (lit. 'keep on being concerned'), but you had no opportunity' (verse 10). It would appear that it was not always easy for the Philippian church to communicate with Paul or to cater for him as they would have desired, but the will was always present even where the deed was out of the question, and as soon as an opportunity opened up they were on their toes to grasp it. This was the spirit of generosity, a truly Christian spirit, which prevailed among them. (*Cf.* Rom. 12: 13; 2 Cor. 9: 1,6,7; 1 Pet. 4: 8,9.) We may take it that this is written for our learning!

As Paul saw it, such a generous sentiment was inseparable from Christian relationships. It was, in fact, *a means of Christian fellowship,* and he commends and approves of it as such. 'It was kind of you', he says, 'to share my trouble' (verse 14). His need was not a remote thing to them. They felt it themselves. It touched them at the point of fellowship, and they responded, and in Paul's estimation (lit.) 'did right nobly' in so acting. It was an 'admirable' thing to do. One member was suffering and all must take note of it (*cf.* 1 Cor. 12: 26,27; Jas. 2: 14–16; 1 Jn. 3: 16–18).

Thirdly, such generosity is *a laying up of treasure in heaven* (verse 17). Paul was always extraordinarily sensitive about receiving monetary help from the churches which he founded, lest anyone should say that he was out for self-advantage (*cf.* 1 Cor. 9). Consequently here, though he clearly needed the help which the Philippians sent, and made no bones about his joy and comfort in receiving it—and indeed (verse 15) showed that he noticed when churches failed to respond to the claims of gratitude towards him—yet, basically, he did not at all covet for himself what they sent, and is even prepared to risk seeming rude in order to emphasize the real value of the gift. His words in verse 17 have the air of an expostulation or a disclaimer, 'Not that I seek the gift.' What a response to an act of sensitive Christian fellowship! But this was not the apostle's intention. It was just that he was so contented to abide by whatever circumstances the Lord appointed for him that he genuinely did not covet their loving alms. But he did covet this, that there should be 'the fruit which increases to your credit' (verse 17). And he seems to suggest that this is a proper motive for Christians to cultivate: they should seek out opportunities to expend their generosity upon the needy, because by selling what they have and giving alms they would make for themselves 'purses that do not grow old . . . a treasure in the heavens that does not fail' (Lk. 12: 33), for God would not be unrighteous and forget their work and the love which they showed toward His name in that they ministered to the saints (Heb. 6: 10).

It is on this note that Paul ends his incidental teaching on Christian generosity. It is *a work acceptable to God,* 'a fragrant offering, a sacrifice acceptable and pleasing to God' (verse 18). There are many references to 'a fragrant offering' in the Bible, but the first sets the scene for the rest and is an ample description of the idea. After the Flood, Noah offered a burnt offering to God, and we read, 'when the Lord smelled the pleasing odour, the Lord said in his heart, "I will never again curse the ground because of man . . ."' (Gn. 8: 21). The picture is homely, the teaching plain. The burnt offering expresses obedient consecration to God, and God delights in the dedication of His people to Himself. Paul teaches here that when Christians take note of Christian needs and extend themselves in generous accommodation to other Christians, it is, for God, the burnt offering all over again, and He delights to accept it.

II CHRISTIAN DISCIPLINE

The first factor, then, which makes for Christian sufficiency or contentment is the generosity of others, as the Lord uses the resources of one to meet the necessities of somebody else. But the second factor in producing contentment is a Christian's own attitude towards circumstances. A Christian may give way to complaint in the dark day, or, on the other hand, he may discipline himself to be content: the discipline of finding sufficiency, no matter what. Paul is speaking personally in these verses, and he opens before us this very thing, that 'sufficiency' and 'contentment' are relative terms—relative to what a person feels himself to need—and *there is a discipline of self whereby one does not need more than one has.*

First of all there must be *the decisive rejection of covetousness.* We have already noted how jealous Paul was to preserve his financial detachment from the rewards of gospel preaching (1 Cor. 9: 18), and how he even endangered the sincerity of his expressions of thanks to the Philippians for their generous gift, 'Not that I complain of want' (verse 11); 'Not that I seek the gift' (verse 17). But in reality he is not giving backhanded or grudging thanks, he is safeguarding the great Christian opposite to covetousness, contentment. The word 'content' (verse 11) had a doubtful past. It had been used by the Stoic philosophers to describe the man of emotionless, wooden impassivity, the man whom nothing could touch because in himself he had found a completely satisfying world. Paul rescued the word and made it mean the 'restful contentment' of the Christian, the opposite of the desire for more. Because he had freed himself from the covetous spirit, he was able to 'ride' every sort of circumstance (verses 11,12). David of old, great man though he was, fell before the temptations of adversity (1 Sa. 27: 1) and of prosperity (2 Sa. 11: 1 ff.) alike. Joseph, earlier on, had triumphed in each arena (Gn. 39: 9; 40: 8). Paul was in the line of Joseph. Circumstances no longer had power to touch him, for he was content.

Such contentment was *something which he learned.* The expression 'I have learned' (verse 11) stresses the personal pronoun, as though Paul was also enquiring whether the Philippians and we ourselves shared his experience, '*I* have learned (have you?)'. When did he learn it, and how? We could understand the verb to speak of a decisive and memorable past event, possibly on the Damascus road or, if 3: 7 refers to some other occasion than that, some experience of Christ which once and for all drove desire for worldly plenty right out of his mind. But it is more likely that he uses this decisive verbal form in order to show what a fixed and unchangeable feature of his character this is. He will never be different. For in the second half of verse 12 he uses another verb, 'I have learned the secret', which was used in the Greek Mystery Religions to describe candidates for admission who had worked their way up through the various lower 'degrees' and had finally been admitted into full possession of 'the mystery' itself. Paul says, 'I have made my way up through the degrees of progressive detachment from the things of the world, its comforts and its discomforts alike, and finally I have reached maturity on this point. I know the secret; circumstances can never again touch me.' Thus contentment is the mark of a mature believer, and the objective to be cultivated by all believers who would grow in Christ who had 'nowhere to lay his head' (Lk. 9: 58).

There is a very interesting comparison of verses concerning the events which took place at Massah, when Israel was journeying from Egypt. In Exodus 17: 7 we read that 'he called the name of the place Massah and Meribah, because of the faultfinding of the children of Israel, and because they put the Lord to the proof by saying, "Is the Lord among us or not?" ' But in Psalm 81: 7 it says, 'I tested you at the waters of Meribah.' Massah and Meribah were not accidents on the way, but purposeful acts of God to 'test' the faith of His people (*cf.* Dt. 8: 2), trying the quality of their devotion to Him. But the people met the test in a spirit of faithlessness. They tried to force God's hand. 'If God were really with us this would never have happened. Let Him deliver us and we will trust Him.' Thus, they 'tested' God. How different was their reaction from the purpose of God! Had they trusted, how trustworthy they would have found Him! Paul had learned the lesson. Bit by bit, test by test, circumstance by circumstance, he persevered through the lower 'degrees' until he finally 'graduated' and the 'secret' was his. Contentment did not come easily. It was purchased at the price of exacting discipline, but, as we shall now see, the end of the matter was gracious, for his heart, weaned away from 'things', was wholly and solely God's.

III CHRISTIAN TRUSTFULNESS

Paul, the contented Christian, gives the sole glory to God. Verse 20 expresses such familiar ideas that we might easily fail to see the wonder of it. What is he giving glory to God about? The times when the Philippians could not help him (verse 10), the times of hunger and of plenty (verse 12), the churches who neglected him and those who remembered him (verse 15)—the totality of his circumstances all accepted as from God, and God glorified in all. Paul was contented because God was trustworthy and to be glorified even when (by worldly standards) He seemed not to be! The apostle had learned to be content because he had learned to trust.

He expresses this in two ways, and, first, in terms of personal experience, 'I can do all things in him who strengthens me' (verse 13). No circumstance could ever arise which would be too much for Paul's God, and therefore no circumstance could ever beat Paul. Here is the vigour of trustfulness. The verse refers to two sorts of power. On the one hand there is the power which Paul experiences in concrete situations of life, 'I am able for all things.' Here is the power which goes out to meet specific circumstances and subdue them. It is the power of victory over the demands of every day. But it arises from another sort of power; it is not inherent in Paul but derivative from elsewhere. Paul has this daily strength for daily needs because of One who (as we might paraphrase) 'endues me with dynamite'. God secretly infuses power (dynamic) into His apostle, and when the need arises it is ready for use.

But the key-word is 'in'. Paul is able only when he is 'in him who strengthens me'. What does this mean? We can illustrate it only by going elsewhere in Scripture. When Israel in Egypt took shelter on Passover night in the houses where the blood of the lamb marked the door, they were, we might say, 'in the lamb', because they were in vital, personal contact with the advantages accruing to them from its death. They sheltered beneath its blood and they fed upon its flesh. So Paul was 'in Christ'—and so are we—by living daily under His sheltering blood and feeding daily and momently upon His flesh (*cf.* Jn. 6: 51–56), that is to say, by preserving a living relationship with the Lamb Himself, our once crucified and now risen Lord, and by living in the good of the benefits which He has purchased for us. This relationship of being 'in Christ', however, is something which we maintain by giving conscious attention to it. Thus, the psalmist wrote, 'Under his wings you will find refuge' (Ps. 91: 4). Here again is a man 'in' God. Just as a chick runs to the mother hen for protection, so he runs to God. In the same way Paul, and we ourselves, are 'in Christ' by fleeing to Him, and pressing close to Him, and covering ourselves in Him, and hiding in Him, by seeing the danger and taking shelter in Him. Finally, we may note John 15: 5–10, for the Lord Jesus Himself spoke of our 'abiding' 'in' Him, and He took care to define what He meant. 'If you abide in me', He said, 'and my words abide in you' (verse 7) . . . 'If you keep my commandments, you will abide in my love' (verse 10). Abiding is conditional upon obedience.

Paul's experience of the trustworthiness of God can therefore be ours. We too can find ability to do all things (meet all circumstances with contentment) 'in' Him who infuses us with dynamic power—if we preserve the preposition 'in' intact. Power arises by constantly and restfully enjoying the benefits of the atonement, constantly and deliberately taking refuge in His proffered security, and constantly and actively living the life of obedience to His words. This sort of trust produces that sort of victory.

Lest, however, we should feel that what Paul expresses in terms of personal experience must be peculiar to him and cannot be our experience as well, he also states the trustworthiness of God in terms of a Christian doctrine, 'My God will supply every need of yours according to his riches in glory in Christ Jesus' (verse 19). The 'all things' of personal experience (verse 13) is matched by the 'every need' which might come upon the Philippians or us. Nothing will prove beyond the capacity of this God whom Paul knows well enough to call '*my* God'. And He will not be niggardly in His supply to them. He 'will supply . . . according to his riches in glory'. He will meet your need to the full and in so doing His supply will not be measured to the dimensions of your need but rather 'according to' (that is, in a manner which befits) His riches. And as if this were not reassurance enough to carry with us into the future there are the added words 'in glory'. It is hard to know precisely what they mean. They may supplement the verb 'supply', 'He will supply . . . in glory', that is 'in glorious measure'. They may describe the riches, He 'will supply in a measure appropriate to His glorious riches'. They may mean 'in the glory (-land)'—all the resources of heaven laid at the disposal of the Christian on earth. Such is the wealth of His supply.

But the key to it all is 'in Christ Jesus'. He is the Mediator to us of all the benefits and blessings of God. More than that, He is Himself the sum of all the blessings, for the preposition is not 'through' but 'in'. He is not a channel along which they flow but a place in which they are deposited. It is finally because of Christ that Paul is contented, and it is Christ whom he offers to us as the means and guarantee of our contentment. For Paul, the person who possessed Christ possessed all.

25 THE RICHNESS OF CHRIST

PAUL BEGAN HIS LETTER TO PHILIPPI in prayer, and he ends in prayer, and his two prayers are identical. 'Grace to you . . . from . . . the Lord Jesus Christ' (1: 2). . . . 'The grace of the Lord Jesus Christ be with your spirit' (4: 23). Nothing could sum up what Paul has been saying better than this observation of the identical prayers. Christ is the *focal point* of the Christian's life, and that in the fullness of His Person and work. He is the Lord, divine and sovereign; He is Jesus, human and exemplary; He is Christ, anointed to be Saviour. This Christ is also the *fountain* of the Christian's life, for from Him is the outpouring of grace, not simply in the initial work and application of salvation but in such a manner that Paul's final benediction can be a simple committal of his friends into the sufficiency of that same grace for whatever of life remains to them. Jesus is the all-sufficient Saviour, Lord, and God.

It would not, of course, be correct to think of the Epistle to the Philippians as more Christ-centred than any of Paul's other writings. They are all on an equality in this, that He is the supreme subject in each and the constantly recurring theme. Philippians, however, is rich in its teaching about the Lord Jesus, and it will be good for us to conclude as Paul did by allowing our gaze to rest exclusively upon Him.

I THE LORD JESUS CHRIST

In Paul's teaching, Jesus is indeed Lord in the fullest sense that the word can convey. In the Old Testament, God revealed to His people Israel His own personal name, which was first expressed by the 'I AM' of Exodus 3: 14, and which then passed into biblical thought as Yahweh, sometimes represented as Jehovah. From motives of extreme reverence for God, however, the use of this name in public speech was considered impossible. The name was too holy for man to dare frame it with his lips, and so people refused the great privilege given to them of calling God by name, and began to substitute for Yahweh a Hebrew noun meaning 'Lord' or 'Sovereign'. Thence it passed into the Greek word, 'Lord' which appears in the New Testament as descriptive of God and, as here, of the Lord Jesus. The title 'Lord', therefore, implies that Jesus is God, and we find in Philippians no suggestion that we should resist the implication, but rather impressive confirmations of it.

In His own Person and Being, Jesus is asserted to be God. The great verse teaching this is 2: 6 where, as we noticed, we may develop the translation in order to reflect the Greek more adequately, 'who, being in origin and by nature in that state which perfectly displays the possession of a divine nature'. In other words, Jesus, in Himself, is God.

But He is also God in the estimation of the Father. It was the Father's good pleasure, in response to the perfection of Calvary, to bestow upon Christ Jesus that supreme exaltation in heaven which could be given only to God (2: 10), for no other *could* be worshipped there but God alone. Along with the position went 'the name which is above every name', which is proclaimed in the universal confession that 'Jesus Christ is *Lord*'. The parallel passage in Isaiah 45: 23 identifies this as the name Yahweh.

Furthermore, Jesus is God in the experience of men. Paul describes himself and Timothy (1: 1) as 'servants of Christ Jesus'. Just as 'the men of God in the old Testament derived their authority from Yahweh, Paul traces back his high calling to *Jesus Christ,* a sure token of his awareness of the Lord's divine nature' (Martin). The same truth is expressed by the conjunction of 'God the Father and the Lord Jesus Christ' as the single source of grace and peace (1: 2). For men also Jesus is God.

II CHRIST OUR RIGHTEOUSNESS

When Paul showed us the Lord Jesus moving out from His native heaven into the world, he concentrated our attention upon the Lord's willing self-denial and obedience. He did not at that point raise the question of the purpose of His leaving of the Father's throne above (2: 5–8). The objective work of saving sinners was not taken up there. But Philippians is rich in teaching about salvation, and we have ventured to sum up its teaching in the word 'righteousness' which appears in the heading, for this seems to be the main emphasis.

The answer to man's desperate need to be 'right' with God is a gift of righteousness which God gives (3: 9). This gift is inseparable from Christ. Paul did not possess it before he possessed Christ (3: 4–7), but being 'found in him' (3: 9) then righteousness—and at that a righteousness which God accepts, for it originated in Him—became Paul's personal possession. He became possessor of this righteousness by simple trust in Christ. In this sense also Christ is the central figure in salvation: not only is the gift ours when we possess Him, but we possess the gift by faith in Him. And this faith, this personal 'leaning' trustfully upon Christ, is no credit or merit of our own. It 'has been granted' to us (1: 29) by Him who 'began a good work' in us (1: 6). Salvation is all of God, and all in Christ.

It is because of this gift of righteousness that we can be entitled 'saints', but lest we should ever permit any wrong feeling or emphasis to tarnish our possession of such a great title, Paul carefully adds the defining words, 'saints *in Christ Jesus*'. Our status before God is solely through Christ. And our continuance before God is equally so. We constantly need grace and find it through Christ (1: 2; 4: 23). Only in Him is there strength (4: 13) and the generous distribution of heavenly riches to meet our present need (4: 19). It is the full supply 'of the Spirit of Jesus Christ' (1: 19) which will carry us through to the final full possession of salvation, and at every moment of the pilgrim way we are as in a castle to which He is the Captain of the Guard, and 'hearts and minds' are kept 'in Christ Jesus' (4: 7).

But those who have received righteousness as a gift from God are expected to display righteousness in their lives, outwardly and inwardly. A pig who claimed to be changed into a boy but who still behaved as a pig would invite only derision and doubt! Those who humbly testify to having received righteousness by faith in Christ must substantiate their profession by their practice. They must bring forth the 'fruit of righteousness'. But even this is Christ-centred and Christ-implemented. The 'fruit of righteousness' is 'through Jesus Christ'. He, the Agent in salvation, is the Agent also in holy productivity.

III SERVANTS OF CHRIST JESUS

What is the relation between the righteousness given to us in Christ and the righteousness which must be seen daily in our lives? The importance of this question is enormous, for it amounts to asking how we may become in experience what we are already in status before God. The foreigner who becomes a naturalized subject may well still have a long way to go before his inner sense of 'belonging' matches that formal recognition of membership which the law has given him, and he may have even further to go before his life thoroughly demonstrates the change of loyalty which his new status involves. Is it not the same for us? We have a heavenly citizenship (3: 20); we have the status of 'saints' (1: 1); God accounts us 'righteous' (3: 9). How does this legal status come to be our conscious inner experience and outward practice?

Paul links the two together by representing the converted man as *active* (*e.g.* 3: 12–14), obedient (2: 12), dedicated (1: 20), and following the example of the Lord Jesus in self-denial (2: 5). It is in the activity of obedient service that we begin to possess our possessions.

The Lord Jesus is the Lord of service. It is He who appoints where and in what manner we shall serve Him. It may mean 'imprisonment' but it will be 'imprisonment . . . for Christ' (1: 13); it may mean plenty to meet all worldly needs, in which case we will 'rejoice in the Lord' (4 : 10) for it will have been His gracious will to raise up those who support us. If our place of service alters, this will be 'in the Lord Jesus', that is, by the appointment of His will (2: 19), and if we make personal plans we must learn to submit them to His overruling, so that our trust for future movements will be 'in the Lord' (2: 23 f.). In other words, we are His bondmen (1: 1).

He is also the power for service, for it is 'in the Lord' that the brethren are 'made confident' (1: 14), and it is 'in the Lord' that the church 'stands firm' against its enemies (4: 1). This is no vain trust, for we are looking to Him to act 'by the power which enables him (that is, even now—not just at the day of His coming) even to subject all things to himself' (3: 21).

The characteristic service of the Christian towards the world is to preach Christ (1: 15,17,18) so that He is the topic of the servant as well as his Lord and his power. The characteristic service of the Christian towards other Christians is to show the example of the Lord Jesus (2: 3–5): thus He is Model, as well as topic, Lord and power. The characteristic resolve of the Christian as he faces the toils and demands and opportunities of the future is to 'make it my own', that is, as RV puts it, to 'apprehend that for which also I was apprehended by Christ Jesus' (3: 12), the express will of Christ as the directive for daily life. But in saying this we have in fact embarked upon yet another aspect of Paul's delineation of Christ, and to this we must now proceed.

IV TO LIVE IS CHRIST

One of the most famous of Paul's sayings occurs in this Epistle, 'to me to live is Christ' (1: 21). From the rest of the Epistle what must we understand this to mean if it is to be true of us as it is of the apostle? It means that we must find all our true joy in Christ (3: 1; 4: 4). It means that we must so exalt Jesus as the only glorious One (3: 3) that we look after the interests of Jesus Christ (2: 21), we continuously grow in the knowledge and appreciation of Him (3 : 7,8), we determine that whatever the future may hold we shall use it to show a life-size portrait of Him to the world (1: 20), not even grudging to risk life itself for His sake (2: 30). It means that we must be content to be made like Him, in His death also (3: 10), accepting suffering such as He appoints for us (1: 29). It means that we shall so seek to follow His example in our dealings with others (2: 5) that we feel towards them with His feelings (1: 8), we assess them as they show themselves to be related to Him (2: 29), and we govern all our attitudes towards them by the consideration that they with us are 'in the Lord' (4: 2) and have their names inscribed in His book (4: 3). It means that we shall take it as our only (1 : 27) task to live worthily of His gospel, and to avoid those ways of life which are opposed to His cross (3: 17,18), and that we shall pursue our course with undeflected gaze fixed upon 'the prize of the upward call of God in Christ Jesus' (3: 14).

For Paul, to whom to live was Christ, He was the focus of all life, the one Object of total dedication, and the single Target at which life aimed. To know Him now, to know Him better by tomorrow, and so to live today and tomorrow as in the end to know Him fully—such was Paul's determined love of his Saviour.

V FOR EVER WITH THE LORD

'In the end to know Him fully': Paul lived this life with a constant eye upon the next. And his appreciation of the Lord sharpened as he contemplated not just the glory which is now Christ's in the heavenlies (2: 9–11; 3: 20,21) but the glory that would be his own in Christ. He speaks here for all Christians and in no sense is he asserting any apostolic privilege in the world to come (*cf.* 2 Tim. 4: 8).

First there is to be noted the personal hope of life with Christ after death. 'To die is gain' (1: 21), that is to say, to die will bring, in one great totality of experience, that fullness of the knowledge of Christ towards which on earth we can but slowly progress. Death to the Christian is no loss, but one colossal profit. The death of a useful Christian may well be a 'loss' to the church he has left behind, but 'no eye has seen, nor ear heard, nor the heart of man conceived' (1 Cor. 2: 9) to imagine the glories that he now possesses. 'To die *is gain*.' The gain is entirely possessed (like the gift of righteousness) in Christ. *He* is the gain, for we 'depart and be with Christ' which is 'by far the best' (see 1: 23). Nothing could be better, says Paul, than to be with Him; there can be no further blessing; this is the ultimate in well-being.

But we may not die. Our earthly life may be terminated in the fulfilment of our expectation from heaven of a Saviour (3: 20). He may come in our lifetime. Thus again Christ fills our awareness of the world to come. Philippians is full of teaching of His coming again. We see it in its certainty, guaranteed by God's declared purpose that every knee shall bow and every tongue confess that Jesus Christ is Lord (2: 9–11). We see it even now being made ready by the constant divine completing of the work of salvation in the individual believer (1: 6). And we see it to be certain in its future fulfilment by reason of His all-victorious power (3: 21). Christ *shall* come again, and with Him He shall bring us all the blessings of the full salvation of which He is the Author, finally making us completely, inwardly and outwardly, into His own glorious image (3: 21).

But the very certainty of the Day of Christ comes home to the Christian with the demand to be ready for such a returning Lord. The tragedy that such a Lord Jesus Christ should come and find us unprepared! Here again is the tension and the unexpected demand in Paul's doctrine of sanctification. When we noted that 'God is at work in you, both to will and to work for his good pleasure' (2: 13) and saw what a fullness of divine inworking was there described, we next found ourselves faced with the command, 'Work out your own salvation' (2: 12). The blessing of the divine inworking is enjoyed by the activity of Christian outworking! Likewise in the doctrine of the Lord's return. God is taking every possible step to make us ready so that when the Day dawns nothing will be amiss, nothing lacking, nothing in short supply (1: 6). What then? Do we therefore become spiritually relaxed, morally unenterprising, because God undertakes all in all? Indeed not so! There is imposed upon us the objective of being '*pure and blameless* for the day of Christ, *filled* with the fruit of *righteousness*' (1: 10,11), and of being fashioned into the 'gently forbearing' likeness of our Lord since He is 'at hand' (4: 5). What could rejoice Him more in the day of His coming than that we had occupied our waiting time in fashioning ourselves into His likeness, so that the Christ who will be our joy for all eternity should be, now also, the completely absorbing and glad objective of holy living and thinking?

So it was, at any rate, for Paul. When he looked up, he saw the reigning Lord Jesus Christ, enthroned at the pinnacle of heaven (2: 9–11). When he looked back, he saw the crucified Lord Jesus Christ, the Christ of Calvary, the Purchaser of salvation and righteousness for all whom He died to save. When he looked forward he saw the returning Lord Jesus Christ, for whose certain coming God would both make him ready and have him prepare himself. When he looked into his own heart, he found there a complete satisfaction in the Lord Jesus Christ. But when he looked at Christ Himself, he saw riches stored up which he had only begun to possess for himself, more of Christ to know, and to gain, more of His fellowship to enjoy, more of His likeness to display, more of His will to learn and to do.

Nothing, then, could supply a more fitting conclusion to Paul's letter to the Philippians than the simplicity of his final prayer, 'The grace of the Lord Jesus Christ be with your spirit.' For himself and for us Paul wanted nothing but daily and deepening experience of the richness of Christ, satisfying and unsearchable.